English Connect

365+

English Connect

365+

Words & Phrases
Second Edition

Eric Thompson

PARTRIDGE

To order additional copies of this book, contact
Toll Free 800 101 2657 (Singapore)
Toll Free 1 800 81 7340 (Malaysia)
orders.singapore@partridgepublishing.com

www.partridgepublishing.com/singapore

INTRODUCTION

This is a collection of useful words and expressions chosen randomly based on long time teaching experience of the author. These words and phrases are just part of the 50,000 frequently used by native speakers. Study one every day, make five sentences (or at least one and come back to make more) of your own, follow the tips in the **treasure boxes,** definitely you'll never be the same after you have finished this book.

The book is designed to be used as a self-study resource for either an active person on the road or at the comfort of home and ready to improve their English vocabulary and conversation skills.

It is useful to jump start you for normal daily conversation or even business interactions.

The idea is to learn **at least** one word per day and make your own sentences in the spaces provided.

Features:

a.   Words or phrases
b.   Meanings
c.   Sample sentences
d.   Spaces for your sentences
e.   Treasure boxes for tips on to becoming fluent in English.
f.   Review sections to keep you update.

If you are really focused and serious about becoming fluent, you should study every day and follow the instructions and tips in the treasure boxes and do not try to finish the book in one day, you will be surprised at the way your English will improve.

Happy Learning!

1. LAZY

Meaning:
A Lazy person is someone who does not like to work hard or does not like to be active.

Examples:
1. She won't work, she's too *lazy*.
2. I've never seen such a *lazy* person before. He lies in bed all day and does nothing.

To understand more look it up in a dictionary. Then make your own sentences below.

1. _____.
2. _____.
3. _____.

2. ILL

Meaning:
To be ill means having a disease or feeling as if your body or mind has been harmed by not being able to work as it should. Not well or unhealthy

Examples:
1. I'm not going to work tomorrow. I'm *ill* and the doctor told me to stay in bed.
2. You're *ill* several times a year. It's time to go to the doctor.

To understand more look it up in a dictionary. Then make your own sentences below.

1. _____.
2. _____.
3. _____.

3. FEVER

Meanings:
a.   It is a body temperature that is higher than normal
b.   It may also mean a state of excited emotion or activity

Examples:
1.   Doctor, I am having a headache, *fever* and cough. Am I having flu?
2.   The whole city seems to be in the football *fever* of EURO 2012.

To understand more look it up in a dictionary. Then make your own sentences below.

1.   _____.

2.   _____.

3.   _____.

4. TO CROSS

Meaning:
To cross means to go from one side of (something) to the other.

Examples:
1.   He was the first runner to *cross* the finish line.
2.   The hunters took 5 days to *cross* the forest.

To understand more look it up in a dictionary. Then make your own sentences below.

1.   _____.

2.   _____.

3.   _____.

5. BRIDGE

Meanings:
a. A structure built over something (such as a river) so that people or vehicles can get across (b)something that joins or connects different people or things

Examples :
1. Let's cross the river here. I think it's the only *bridge* in the village.
2. Her work serves as a *bridge* between the past and the present.

To understand more look it up in a dictionary. Then make your own sentences below.

1. _____.

2. _____.

3. _____.

6. TO BURN

Meanings:
To destroy or damage something by fire or heat.

Examples:
1. The fire started at 6 p.m. and the whole city was *burning* after only 4 hours.
2. If you play with the matches, you will *burn* yourself!

To understand more look it up in a dictionary. Then make your own sentences below.

1. _____.

2. _____.

3. _____.

7. ECONOMY

Meaning:
The process or system by which goods and services are produced, sold, and bought in a country or region.

Examples:
1. The government should improve the state of the *economy.*
2. The high unemployment resulted from the *economy* crisis of 2008-09.

To understand more look it up in a dictionary. Then make your own sentences below.

1. _____.
2. _____.
3. _____.

8. TECHNIQUE

Meaning:
A way of doing something by using special knowledge or skill.

Examples:
1. I want to practice some new photographic *technique.*
2. Psychologists develop new learning *techniques.*

To understand more look it up in a dictionary. Then make your own sentences below.

1. _____.
2. _____.
3. _____.

9. COMPLIMENT

Meaning:
A remark that says something good about someone or something

Examples:
1. What a lovely dress! Oh, thanks for the *compliment.*
2. He couldn't take his eyes off her and was telling her many *compliments* at the party.

To understand more look it up in a dictionary. Then make your own sentences below.

1. _____.
2. _____.
3. _____.

10. SMOKE

Meaning;
The cloud of black, gray, or white gases and dust that is produced by burning something

Examples:
1. There was a lot of *smoke* coming from the bonfire made by our neighbors.
2. Do you mind if I *smoke* here? No, I'd rather you go out, I can't stand the cigarette smoke.

To understand more look it up in a dictionary. Then make your own sentences below.

1. _____.
2. _____.
3. _____.

11. TO NOTICE

Meaning:
This word means to become aware of something or someone by seeing, hearing, etc.

Examples:
1. She had a new blouse, but her husband didn't even *notice* it.
2. I *noticed* that they were looking rather nervous and asked them what had happened.

To understand more look it up in a dictionary. Then make your own sentences below.

1. _____.
2. _____.
3. _____.

12. STRANGER

Meaning:
A stranger is someone who is neither a friend nor an acquaintance.

Examples:
1. A tall, dark-skinned *stranger* waved to me in front of the shop. Do you know him?
2. The quietness of the village was disturbed by the arrival of the *stranger* from an unknown land.

To understand more look it up in a dictionary. Then make your own sentences below.

1. _____.
2. _____.
3. _____.

13. TO BREAK

Meaning:
To break is to cause separation into pieces suddenly or violently.

Examples:
1. I dropped the glasses and they all *broke*, making a lot of noise and mess.
2. They died in the mountains when their rope suddenly *broke*.

To understand more look it up in a dictionary. Then make your own sentences below.

1. _____.

2. _____.

3. _____.

14. SPEAK UP

Meanings:
1. To speak loud enough to be audible.
2. To speak without fear or hesitation.

Examples:
1. *Speak up* please, because people at the back can't hear you.
2. If you disagree with the others, you should *speak up* now.

To understand more look it up in a dictionary. Then make your own sentences below.

1. _____.

2. _____.

3. _____.

15. SUDDEN

Meaning:
Something is sudden when it is happening, coming, or done very quickly in a way that is usually not expected.

Examples:
1. His *sudden* illness made us cancel our trip to Paris.
2. There was a *sudden* increase in the price of oil.

To understand more look it up in a dictionary. Then make your own sentences below.

1. _____.

2. _____.

3. _____.

TREASURE BOX1: MAKE SENTENCES

> Make <u>at least</u> one sentence of your own after each word or phrase. It will help you retain what you have learned and to be able to reproduce it when you will need to do so.

16. RECOMMEND

Meaning:
When you recommend something or someone you say that someone or something is good and deserves to be chosen.

Examples:
1. Can you *recommend* me a good place to go on holidays?
2. I *recommend* that you read this book if you want to pass the exam. You'll find the most important facts there.

To understand more look it up in a dictionary. Then make your own sentences below.

1. _____.

2. _____.

3. _____.

17. SURVIVE

Meaning:
To remain alive or in existence or to continue to live or exist, especially after coming close to dying or being destroyed or after being in a difficult or threatening situation.

Examples:
1. Four people were killed in the accident; she was the only one to *survive*.
2. They somehow managed to *survive* the difficult time of the war.

To understand more look it up in a dictionary. Then make your own sentences below.

1. _____.

2. _____.

3. _____.

18. DECLARE

Meaning:
To make something known formally or officially or to say something in a strong and confident way.

Examples:
1. Do you have anything to *declare*?
2. She was *declared* the winner of the first prize.

To understand more look it up in a dictionary. Then make your own sentences below.

1. _____.
2. _____.
3. _____.

19. RICH

Meaning:
To have great abundant supply of something or to possess great material wealth.

Examples:
1. She married him, because he's *rich* and able to give her everything she'd always dreamt about.
2. Fruits are *rich* in vitamins.

To understand more look it up in a dictionary. Then make your own sentences below.

1. _____.
2. _____.
3. _____.

20. INSERT

Meaning:
To put something in something or to be involved or to involve someone in an activity.

Examples:
1. The light went out and I had difficulties to *insert* the key in the lock.
2. They tried to *insert* themselves into the conversation.

To understand more look it up in a dictionary. Then make your own sentences below.

1. _____.

2. _____.

3. _____.

Exercise 1

Choose the correct definition for the words below:

1. Fever.
   a. Hostile or unfriendly.
   b. A rise in the temperature of the body; frequently a symptom of infection.
   c. Something that reflects in an unfavorable way on one.

2. Economy.
   a. Intense nervous anticipation; «in a fever of resentment.
   b. The system of production and distribution and consumption
   c. Something that reflects in an unfavorable way on one.

3. Smoke.
   a. Something that causes suffering.
   b. Something that reflects in an unfavorable way on one.
   c. A cloud of fine particles suspended in a gas.

4. To survive.
   a. Continue to live through hardship or adversity.
   b. Resulting in suffering.
   c. To separate into components or parts.

5. Ill
   a. To exist or support oneself.
   b. To cause to separate into pieces suddenly or violently.
   c. Not healthy or sick.

6. To burn.
   a. To undergo rapid combustion or consume fuel in such a way as to give off heat.
   b. Continue to live through hardship or adversity.
   c. To cause to separate into pieces suddenly or violently.

7. Technique.
    a. To live past a life-threatening event.
    b. To feel strong emotion or passion.
    c. A practical method or art applied to some particular task.

8. Bridge.
    a. A specific method of production.
    b. A structure that allows people or vehicles to cross an obstacle such as a river or canal or railway etc.
    c. To force or make a way through, puncture or penetrate.

9. To cross.
    a. To connect or reduce the distance between objects.
    b. To intersect or meet at a point.
    c. To force or make a way through, puncture or penetrate.

10. Sudden.
    a. To feel extreme anger.
    b. To become separated into pieces or fragments.
    c. Happening without warning or in a short space of time.

EXERCISE 2

Choose the best words for the following definitions:

1. A movement from one place to another.
   a. Fever
   b. To notice
   c. Cross
   d. Ill

2. A warning or intimation of something.
   a. Technique
   b. Smoke
   c. To notice
   d. Sudden

3. An expression of esteem, respect, affection, or admiration.
   a. Compliment
   b. Stranger
   c. To recommend
   d. To survive.

4. A person or thing that is unknown or with whom one is unacquainted.
   a. Compliment.
   b. Stranger
   c. Economy
   d. Rich

5. To present as worthy of acceptance or trial.
   a. Rich
   b. Recommend
   c. To survive
   d. To assist.

6. To convey thoughts, opinions, or emotions orally.
   a. To insert
   b. To speak up
   c. To notice
   d. To break

7. To make something known formally or officially.
   a. To assist
   b. To insert
   c. To declare
   d. To compliment

8. To put or set into, between, or among.
   a. To hire
   b. To assist
   c. To insert
   d. To speak up

9. Possessing great material wealth.
   a. Hire
   b. Assist
   c. Rich
   d. Brand

10. Payment for labor or services to a worker, especially remuneration on an hourly daily or weekly basis or by the piece.
    a. Hire
    b. Wage
    c. Quality
    d. Consult

21. QUALITY

Meaning:
Quality means the standard of something as measured against other things of a similar kind. Simply put, it means how good or bad something is.

Examples:
1. I won't visit this restaurant again. The food is of such a poor *quality*.
2. If you buy top *quality* products with a lifelong guarantee, you have to pay more.

To understand more look it up in a dictionary. Then make your own sentences below.

1. _____.
2. _____.
3. _____.

22. ASSIST

Meaning:
To assist means to give support or help in various ways such as by giving information, money or doing a share of the work.

Examples:
1. We are expected to *assist* the guests with interpreting during the conference and their free time.
2. Foreign armies arrived to *assist* in restoring peace.

To understand more look it up in a dictionary. Then make your own sentences below.

1. _____.
2. _____.
3. _____.

23. HIRE

Meaning:
Obtain the temporary use of (something) for an agreed payment or to give work or a job to (someone) in exchange for wages or a salary

Examples:
1. How much does it cost to *hire* a car for 2 days?
2. He was *hired* for a short period of time to help with the new project.

To understand more look it up in a dictionary. Then make your own sentences below.

1. _____.
2. _____.
3. _____.

24. WAGES

Meaning:
A wage is a fixed regular payment earned for work or services, typically paid on a daily or weekly basis.

Examples:
1. Graduating from university cannot guarantee high *wages* nowadays.
2. She's too proud to work for low *wages*.

To understand more look it up in a dictionary. Then make your own sentences below.

1. _____.
2. _____.
3. _____.

25. MULTINATIONAL COMPANY

Meaning:
A multinational corporation (MNC) has facilities and other assets in at least one country other than its home country.

Example:
Many multinational companies set up their subsidiaries in Asia to benefit from its cheap labor force.

To understand more look it up in a dictionary. Then make your own sentences below.

1. _____.
2. _____.
3. _____.

26. COMPETITIVE

Meaning:
Competitive situation is when people or groups are trying to win a contest or be more successful than others.

Examples:
1. Football/Soccer is one of the most *competitive* sports in the world.
2. The market of electronic devices is very *competitive* because of high innovation.

To understand more look it up in a dictionary. Then make your own sentences below.

1. _____.
2. _____.
3. _____.

27. BRAND AWARENESS

Meaning:
Brand awareness is the possibility that consumers recognize the existence and availability of a company's product or service.

Examples:
1. The key to success of a brand is to build ***brand awareness*** among customers.
2. People easily associate Nokia with mobile phones and Levis with jeans due to the high ***brand awareness.***

To understand more look it up in a dictionary. Then make your own sentences below.

1. _____.

2. _____.

3. _____.

28. CLASSIC BRAND

Meaning:
A Classic brand is a well-known brand with a long history.

Examples:
1. Levis is perceived as a ***classic brand*** in the clothing market.
2. People often choose ***classic brands*** that they've known for ages, because they seem reliable for them.

To understand more look it up in a dictionary. Then make your own sentences below.

1. _____.

2. _____.

3. _____.

29. ZEBRA CROSSING

Meaning:
It is a place on a road, especially one where there is a lot of traffic, across which wide, black and white lines are painted, and at which vehicles must stop to allow people to walk across the road

Examples:
1. Many people die each day, because they don't cross roads on *zebra crossing*.
2. I failed my driving test, because I forgot to slow down before *zebra crossing*.

To understand more look it up in a dictionary. Then make your own sentences below.

1. _____.

2. _____.

3. _____.

30. TO REDUCE

Meaning:
To reduce is to make something smaller in size, amount or number.

Examples:
1. Our company really needs to *reduce* expenses at this difficult time.
2. Many shops *reduce* their prices before Christmas to attract customers.

To understand more look it up in a dictionary. Then make your own sentences below.

1. _____.

2. _____.

3. _____.

TREASURE BOX 2: USE YOUR DICTIONARY

I strongly recommend using a paper English-English dictionary when you study on your own. Many teachers have noticed that their students remember words much longer when they search for them in the paper dictionary. Also, dictionaries in book form generally give more detail examples than electronic dictionaries.

31. COMMERCIAL

Meaning:
The term is also widely used in other areas of finance and everyday life, it generally means an activity that pertains to business or one that has a profit motive.

Examples:
1. What drives me mad while watching films is a *commercial* break every 20 minutes.
2. *Commercials* are the main source of media income.

To understand more look it up in a dictionary. Then make your own sentences below.

1. _____.

2. _____.

3. _____.

32. TO CONSULT

Meaning:
To consult is to ask for the professional opinion of someone in order to make a decision.

Examples:
1. If you have any problem with the project, please *consult* our experts.
2. I have no idea of how to get there. I'll *consult* the map.

To understand more look it up in a dictionary. Then make your own sentences below.

1. _____.
2. _____.
3. _____.

33. CHEERFUL

Meaning:
To be cheerful is feeling or showing happiness or showing that you are willing to do something without complaining

Examples:
1. In spite of his numerous problems he's always *cheerful*.
2. After having a bad day I like listening to some *cheerful* music.

To understand more look it up in a dictionary. Then make your own sentences below.

1. _____.
2. _____.
3. _____.

34. COMMODITY

Meaning:
Something useful or valuable that can be bought or sold.

Examples:
1. People are afraid that **commodity** prices will rise if we enter the Euro zone.
2. Farmers are happy, because the demand for agricultural **commodities** has risen recently.

To understand more look it up in a dictionary. Then make your own sentences below.

1. _____.

2. _____.

3. _____.

35. TO PRODUCE

Meaning:
To produce something means to make, compose, create, or bring out by intellectual or physical effort.

Examples:
1. His company *produces* mobile phones.
2. There's a slump in *producing* luxury goods, because people don't buy as many of them as in the past.

To understand more look it up in a dictionary. Then make your own sentences below.

1. _____.

2. _____.

3. _____.

36. MODEST

Meaning:
To be modest is having or showing a moderate estimation of one's own abilities, accomplishments, or value and of something.

Examples:
1. She was so *modest* about her success. She said that it was nothing extraordinary.
2. He's rich but *modest*. He never makes the other feel worse.

To understand more look it up in a dictionary. Then make your own sentences below.

1. _____.
2. _____.
3. _____.

37. CRUEL

Meaning:
To be cruel means to be extremely unkind and unpleasant and causing pain to people or animals intentionally.

Examples:
Vegetarians claim that eating animals is *cruel*.

To understand more look it up in a dictionary. Then make your own sentences below.

1. _____.
2. _____.
3. _____.

38. SINCERE

Meaning:
Sincere means having or showing true feelings that are expressed in an honest way.

Examples:
1. I'm sure he was not *sincere* in what he said to me last night. He often tells lies.
2. He's a great actor. He's so *sincere* in what he does!

To understand more look it up in a dictionary. Then make your own sentences below.

1. _____.
2. _____.
3. _____.

39. QUARREL

Meaning:
A *quarrel* is an angry argument between two or more friends or family members or countries.

Examples:
1. After a *quarrel* they decided to split up.
2. Our neighbors *quarrel* all the time, preventing me from falling asleep.

To understand more look it up in a dictionary. Then make your own sentences below.

1. _____.
2. _____.
3. _____.

40. ORDINARY

Meaning:
When something or situation is ordinary it means it is not different or it is of no special quality or interest in any way unusual.

Examples:
1. They've got an *ordinary* sort of house, it's really nothing special.
2. People wake up every morning to start another *ordinary* day.

To understand more look it up in a dictionary. Then make your own sentences below.

1. _____.

2. _____.

3. _____.

EXERCISE 3

Choose the best word for the following definitions:

1. Having a happy feeling; in good spirits.
   a. Wages
   b. Commercial
   c. Consult
   d. Cheerful

2. To seek advice or information.
   a. To reduce
   b. To consult
   c. To notice
   d. To hire

3. To manufacture or create economic goods and services.
   a. To produce
   b. To reduce
   c. To recommend
   d. To survive

4. Not hypocritical or deceitful; open; genuine.
   a. Competitive
   b. Quality
   c. Sincere
   d. Cruel

5. Free from showiness or ostentation; unpretentious
   a. Assist
   b. Recommend
   c. Modest
   d. Rich.

6. Something useful that can be turned to commercial or other advantage
   a. Commodity.
   b. Commercial
   c. Competitive
   d. Economy

7. To engage the services of (a person) for a fee.
   a. To hire
   b. To assist
   c. To insert
   d. To compliment

8. To give aid or support.
   a. To cross
   b. To assist
   c. To hire
   d. To speak up

9. Degree or grade of excellence.
   a. Commercial
   b. Quality
   c. Rich
   d. Commodity

10. To bring down amount, or degree; diminish.
    a. To declare
    b. To hug
    c. To produce
    d. To reduce

EXERCISE 4

Choose the best word for the following definitions:

1. An angry dispute; a disagreement marked by a temporary or permanent break in friendly relationship.
   a. Cruel
   b. Modest.
   c. Quarrel

2. To deduct a certain amount from a bill, charge, etc.
   a. To reduce
   b. To consult
   c. To discount

3. To breathe during sleep with hoarse or harsh sounds.
   a. To survive
   b. To snore
   c. To sneeze

4. To look with winking or half-shut eyes.
   a. Dive
   b. Blink
   c. Examine

5. To actively and attentively engage in work or a pastime.
   a. Busy
   b. Consult
   c. Assist

6. Something offensive or annoying to individuals or to the community.
   a. Rotten
   b. Quarrel
   c. Nuisance

7. Something that is plain, not special or undistinguished.
   a. Assist
   b. Spot
   c. Ordinary

8. A complete in natural growth or development, as plant and animal forms.
   a. Sincere
   b. Mature
   c. Superior

9. An approximate judgment or calculation, as of the value, amount, time, size, or weight of something
   a. Quality
   b. Brand
   c. Estimate

10. To give back or restore, especially money.
    a. Refund
    b. Review
    c. Repeat

41. HUG

Meaning:
To hug is to put your arms around someone especially as a way of showing love or friendship.

Examples:
1. She *hugged* him tightly, because she really missed him.
2. The mother *hugged* the child after he apologized to her for his bad behavior.

To understand more look it up in a dictionary. Then make your own sentences below.

1. _____.

2. _____.

3. _____.

42. NUISANCE

Meaning:
A nuisance is a person, thing, or situation that is annoying or that causes trouble or problems.

Examples:
1. The new neighbor is becoming a **nuisance**, dropping in on us several times a day.
2. Folding up this map correctly is such a **nuisance**.

To understand more look it up in a dictionary. Then make your own sentences below.

1. _____.

2. _____.

3. _____.

43. INDECISIVE

Meaning:
To be indecisive is the inability to make choices quickly and confidently.

Examples:
1. I can't stand his *indecisive* answers! I never know what's going on in his mind.
2. She didn't get this job, because she was so *indecisive* during the job interview.

To understand more look it up in a dictionary. Then make your own sentences below.

1. _____.
2. _____.
3. _____.

44. MATURE

Meaning:
To mature refers to someone or something having or showing the mental and emotional qualities of an adult or to be at the final or desired state of growth.

Examples:
1. He's only 15, but his *mature* approach to life is unbelievable.
2. She *matured* her songwriting skill throughout her career.

To understand more look it up in a dictionary. Then make your own sentences below.

1. _____.
2. _____.
3. _____.

45. BUSY

Meaning:
To be busy means to be actively and attentively engaged doing something.

Examples:
1. Since he took up his new job, he's been extremely *busy* and has no time for friends and family.
2. Are we going to the cinema tonight? No, sorry, I'm *busy*. I have to finish this project for tomorrow.

To understand more look it up in a dictionary. Then make your own sentences below.

1. _____.

2. _____.

3. _____.

TREASURE BOX 3: AVOID TRANSLATION

When you discuss in English, you need to imagine a lot and avoid translating into your native language in your head to be able to keep up with your discussion.

46. TO SPOT

Meaning:
To spot means to see or notice someone or something that is difficult to see or find.

Example:
He *spotted* me in the crowd at the concert.

To understand more look it up in a dictionary. Then make your own sentences below.

1. _____.

2. _____.

3. _____.

47. TO EXAMINE

Meaning:
To examine is to look at something, situation or someone closely and carefully in order to learn more or to find problems.

Examples:
1. Every luggage will be *examined* at the airport.
2. Several doctors *examined* him thoroughly, but none of them found the cause of his migraines.

To understand more look it up in a dictionary. Then make your own sentences below.

1. _____.

2. _____.

3. _____.

48. To Bleed

Meaning:
To bleed is to lose or release blood internally into the body or externally because of a cut or injury.

Examples:
1. I fell from the stairs and my leg was *bleeding* heavily.
2. Your hand is *bleeding*, what happened? I accidentally cut myself with a knife.

To understand more look it up in a dictionary. Then make your own sentences below.

1. _____.
2. _____.
3. _____.

49. Bump Into

Meaning:
To bump into someone is to meet someone you know when you have not planned to meet them or to find something unexpectedly.

Examples:

1. What a surprise! I *bumped* into John when I was in Los Angeles.
2. I was fired, because I *bumped* into my boss in the pub, whereas I should have been ill in hospital.

To understand more look it up in a dictionary. Then make your own sentences below.

1. _____.
2. _____.
3. _____.

50. TO SNORE

Meaning:
To snore is to breathe in a very noisy way while you are sleeping.

Examples:
1. I can't sleep at night, because my husband *snores* terribly.
2. We knew that he was already asleep, because we could hear him *snoring*.

To understand more look it up in a dictionary. Then make your own sentences below.

1. _____.
2. _____.
3. _____.

51. TO SUCK

Meaning:
To suck is to pull in liquid or air through your mouth without using your teeth, or to move the tongue and muscles of the mouth around something inside your mouth, often in order to dissolve it.

Examples :
1. Don't *suck* so many sweets, or you'll have to go to the dentist!
2. The sleeping baby was *sucking* its thumb.

To understand more look it up in a dictionary. Then make your own sentences below.

1. _____.
2. _____.
3. _____.

52. TO SNEEZE

Meaning:
When you sneeze, air and often small drops of liquid suddenly and forcefully come out of your nose and mouth in a way you cannot control:

Examples:
1. I had to sell the cat, because it made me *sneeze*. I think I'm allergic to the fur.
2. You're *sneezing* all the time. Did you catch a cold?

To understand more look it up in a dictionary. Then make your own sentences below.

1. _____.
2. _____.
3. _____.

53. TO BLINK

Meaning:
When you blink, you close and then open your eyes quickly once or several times.

Examples:
1. He *blinked* when he came out into the light of the day.
2. *Blink* several times to get the lash out of your eye.

To understand more look it up in a dictionary. Then make your own sentences below.

1. _____.
2. _____.
3. _____.

54. REFUND

Meaning:
A refund is an amount of money that is given back to you, especially because you are not happy with a product or service that you have bought

Examples:
1. I took the computer back to the shop and I was given a *refund*.
2. I was not satisfied with the trip, so the travel agency decided to give me 50% *refund*.

To understand more look it up in a dictionary. Then make your own sentences below.

1. _____.
2. _____.
3. _____.

55. CHALLENGE

Meaning:
A situation or something that needs great mental or physical effort in order to be successful or a call to compete.

Examples:
1. It was a very difficult task but she rose to the *challenge*.
2. Bribery is one of the biggest *challenges* that the government has to deal with.

To understand more look it up in a dictionary. Then make your own sentences below.

1. _____.
2. _____.
3. _____.

56. DISCOUNT

Meaning:
A discount is an amount taken off a regular price.

Examples:
1. If you buy more than one exemplar, you'll get a *discount* of 15%.
2. Polish railways offer 33% *discount* for students.

To understand more look it up in a dictionary. Then make your own sentences below.

1. _____.

2. _____.

3. _____.

57. SUPERIOR

Meaning:
Someone or something that is better than average or better than other people or things of the same type is said to be superior.

Examples:
1. The worker was reported to his *superiors* for being frequently late for work.
2. I'm sure this marvelous painting is of a *superior* artist.

To understand more look it up in a dictionary. Then make your own sentences below.

1. _____.

2. _____.

3. _____.

58. STORAGE

Meaning:
A storage is the space where you put things when they are not being used.

Examples:
1. Our furniture will remain in the *storage* until we find a new house.
2. The goods are all in our *storage* and we are ready to send them to you if you buy them on the Internet.

To understand more look it up in a dictionary. Then make your own sentences below.

1. _____.
2. _____.
3. _____.

59. DIVE

Meaning:
To dive is to jump into water, especially with your head and arms going in first, or to swim underwater usually while using special equipment to help you breathe.

Examples:
1. She made a graceful dive into the pool.
2. They are diving to find treasure from the Italian shipwreck.

To understand more look it up in a dictionary. Then make your own sentences below.

1. _____.
2. _____.
3. _____.

60. To Scratch

Meaning:

This word means to cut or damage a surface or your skin slightly with or on something sharp or rough.

Examples:

1. I left my car near the forest and I found it in the morning with the roof *scratched* heavily by the falling branches.
2. He now has a very successful business but he started from *scratch*.

To understand more look it up in a dictionary. Then make your own sentences below.

1. _____.

2. _____.

3. _____.

TREASURE BOX 4: PRACTICE, PRACTICE, PRACTICE !

Practice makes perfection; you have to practice, Practice, Practice, as much as you can if you really want to be fluent in English Language. Listen a lot. Listen to real English on TV or Radio and get used to native speakers` way of speaking and try to imitate them while you **cook** yours.

EXERCISE 5

Choose the best words for the following definitions:

1. To observe carefully or critically.
   a. To Exchange
   b. To Examine
   c. To Consult

2. To hold steadfastly to; cherish.
   a. To Bump into
   b. To Estimate
   c. To Hug

3. Being in a state of putrefaction or decay; decomposed.
   a. Rotten
   b. Spot
   c. Nuisance

4. To plunge, especially headfirst, into water
   a. Dive
   b. Blink
   c. Examine

5. To use the nails or claws to dig or scrape at.
   a. To Suck
   b. To Bleed
   c. To Scratch

6. Of a higher nature or kind.
   a. Quality
   b. Superior
   c. Challenge

7. To expel air forcibly from the mouth and nose in an explosive action.
   a. To Sneeze
   b. To Spot
   c. To Snore

8. A space for storing goods.
   a. Storage
   b. Mature
   c. Superior

9. To emit or lose blood.
   a. To Suck
   b. To Bleed
   c. To Estimate

10. A call to engage in a contest, fight, or competition.
    a. To Suck
    b. To Challenge
    c. To Compete

EXERCISE 6 (BONUS EXERCISE)

Fill in the gaps with the best answers from a- c.

1. Go to the _____ and try this dress on.
    [a] checkout
    [b] exchange
    [c] changing room

2. Look at the _____ ! This shirt is too expensive.
    You can't afford it.
    [a] price tag
    [b] size
    [c] shopping list

3. I've lost my _____ but I'd like to return this scarf.
    Is it possible?
    [a] afford
    [b] shopping list
    [c] receipt

4. I would like to return this electric kettle. Can I have a _____?
    [a] price tag
    [b] refund
    [c] checkout

5. May I try it on? - Yes, what _____ are you?
    [a] try on
    [b] size
    [c] shopper

6. I'd like to get a _____ for these shoes because they are too tight.
   [a] refund
   [b] size
   [c] try on

7. There was a big sale at that mall last week. Many _____ arrived at 4 a.m. to ensure a good place in line.
   [a] shopper
   [b] shoppers
   [c] fitting room

8. We go to the _____ because it sells products at lower prices.
   [a] changing room
   [b] discount store
   [c] afford

9. Henry lost his _____ and forgot to buy pork loin.
   [a] receipt
   [b] refund
   [c] shopping list

10. She worked on the _____ at the supermarket last summer.
    [a] checkout
    [b] discount store
    [c] changing room

11. Have you got this dress in black? - Yes, we have. - Can I _____?
    [a] try it on
    [b] exchange
    [c] refund

12. I missed my train because I was queuing at the _____
    in a supermarket.
    [a] checkout
    [b] size
    [c] receipt

13. I bought this sweater yesterday but it's too small. Can I _____
    it please?
    [a] checkout
    [b] exchange
    [c] receipt

14. We don't have enough money. We aren't able to _____
    such expensive shoes.
    [a] exchange
    [b] afford
    [c] refund

15. Where can I try the jeans on? The _____ is over
    there.
    [a] discount store
    [b] fitting room
    [c] price tag

16. This jacket _____ you very well. I think you should
    buy it.
    [a] suit
    [b] suits
    [c] sizes

17. This tailcoat was very expensive but Ted could still _____ it.
    [a] suit
    [b] refund
    [c] afford

18. You spend too much on clothes. Don't you look at the _____ before buying something?
    [a] size
    [b] price tag
    [c] changing room

19. I'm going to buy her the blue dress. This color _____ her best.
    [a] suits
    [b] tries on
    [c] refunds

20. If you don't like the color of the pullover, you can _____ it. You'll get another one.
    [a] receipt
    [b] checkout
    [c] exchange

61. ROTTEN

Meaning:
Something is rotten when it is very bad, unpleasant or decayed and no longer useful.

Examples:
1. A: What's that terrible stink? B: It's the *rotten* eggs.
2. The lizards live in cool, dark places such as *rotten* logs

To understand more look it up in a dictionary. Then make your own sentences below.

1. _____.
2. _____.
3. _____.

62. TO ESTIMATE

Meaning:
To estimate is to guess based on the information you have about the size, amount, etc., of something.

Example:
I tried to *estimate* how far the town is, but it was difficult because the map was not very precise.

To understand more look it up in a dictionary. Then make your own sentences below.

1. _____.
2. _____.
3. _____.

63. ACCESSIBLE

Meaning:
Something or someone is accessible if they are easy to be reached or approached

Examples:
1. The city is *accessible* only by boat or plane.
2. The book is not *accessible* for children below 12.

To understand more look it up in a dictionary. Then make your own sentences below.

1. _____.
2. _____.
3. _____.

64. TO PRONOUNCE

Meaning:
To pronounce means to say a word or a letter in a particular way or in a correct way:

Examples:
1. Don't *pronounce* the letter "k" in the word "know".
2. Sorry, I didn't catch your name, could you *pronounce* it?

To understand more look it up in a dictionary. Then make your own sentences below.

1. _____.
2. _____.
3. _____.

65. CONVENIENT

Meaning:
Something is convenient when it is suitable for your purposes and causing no difficulty for your schedule or plans:

Example:
The room is very *convenient* because of all its useful electronic devices.

To understand more look it up in a dictionary. Then make your own sentences below.

1. _____.
2. _____.
3. _____.

66. TO TRANSMIT

Meaning:
To send or give something or to broadcast or carry signals using radio or television.

Examples:
1. My favorite program wasn't *transmitted* yesterday because of bad weather conditions.
2. The disease *transmitted* incredibly fast, killing every person that was affected.

To understand more look it up in a dictionary. Then make your own sentences below.

1. _____.
2. _____.
3. _____.

67. TROUBLESOME

Meaning:
Something is troublesome when it is causing a lot of problems for someone:

Examples:
1. I'm going to the dentist today with my *troublesome* tooth.
2. She has so many problems with her *troublesome* children.

To understand more look it up in a dictionary. Then make your own sentences below.

1. _____.

2. _____.

3. _____.

68. SUPERFICIAL

Meaning:
Superficial is concerned only with what is obvious or not deep.

Example:
a. They had a *superficial* knowledge or understanding of the topic.
b. The storm only caused *superficial* damage to the building.
c. Despite a *superficial* resemblance, the paintings are by two different artists.

To understand more look it up in a dictionary. Then make your own sentences below.

1. _____.

2. _____.

3. _____.

69. COLLABORATE

Meaning:
This word means to work with another person or group in order to achieve something.

Examples:
1. They are *collaborating* with Microsoft on the new software.
2. He was accused of *collaborating* with the enemy and was sentenced to death.

To understand more look it up in a dictionary. Then make your own sentences below.

1. _____.

2. _____.

3. _____.

70. STROLL

Meaning:
To stroll is to walk in a slow, relaxed manner, especially for pleasure.

Examples:
1. I love *strolling* on the beach in the early morning. It's so relaxing.
2. Tourists *stroll* in the streets of holiday resorts the whole summer.

To understand more look it up in a dictionary. Then make your own sentences below.

1. _____.

2. _____.

3. _____.

71. To Demoralize

Meaning:
To demoralize means to take away the confidence and courage of a person or persons.

Examples:
1. The company's inconsistent policy has **demoralized** the staff.
2. Japan has determined not to be **demoralized** by the earthquake.

To understand more, look it up in a dictionary. Then make your own sentences below.

1. _____.
2. _____.
3. _____.

72. Distinctive

Meaning:
If something is distinctive it has a special quality, style and attractiveness.

Examples:
1. It's easy to recognize him from distance because of his **distinctive** way of walking.
2. I think I wouldn't recognize him on the street, he isn't a very **distinctive** person.

To understand more look it up in a dictionary. Then make your own sentences below.

1. _____.
2. _____.
3. _____.

73. WITHDRAW MONEY

Meaning:
To withdraw money from an account is to remove money from an account.

Examples:
1. You may **withdraw** $300 from your account each day from cash dispensers.
2. Somebody had stolen my credit cards and I found out later that all my money was **withdrawn** from my accounts

To understand more look it up in a dictionary. Then make your own sentences below.

1. _____.
2. _____.
3. _____.

74. DEPOSIT MONEY

Meaning:
Something, such as money, that is entrusted for safekeeping, in a bank or to give (money) in part payment or as security

Example:
I paid $10 as a **deposit** so that the shop assistant could keep the jacket for me until the next day.

To understand more look it up in a dictionary. Then make your own sentences below.

1. _____.
2. _____.
3. _____.

75. ACCELERATE

Meaning:
To accelerate is to cause faster development, progress in process or situation.

Examples:
1. The car *accelerated* to overtake the truck.
2. The country's annual inflation *accelerated* up to 3% in March.

To understand more look it up in a dictionary. Then make your own sentences below.

1. _____.

2. _____.

3. _____.

TREASURE BOX 5: KEEP IT SIMPLE AND SHORT.

This means that you should not try to explain yourself in long sentences all the time. When you keep it simple and short,

a. You will go straight to the point.

b. You will save yourself the headache of explaining.

c. You will not confuse yourself and your listener.

d. You will save your time and your listener's.

76. LANDLORD

Meaning:
A landlord is a person or organization that owns and leases apartments to others.

Examples:
After the students had thrown a big party, the *landlord* broke the contract and ordered them to leave his flat in 3 days.

To understand more look it up in a dictionary. Then make your own sentences below.

1. _____.
2. _____.
3. _____.

77. TENANT

Meaning:
A person or group that rents and occupies land, ahouse, an office, or the like, from another for a period of time.

Examples:
1. The rents are getting bigger and the number of *tenants* is falling down.
2. *Tenants* are real victims of the economic recession because their payments are getting smaller, whereas their rents are not.

To understand more look it up in a dictionary. Then make your own sentences below.

1. _____.
2. _____.
3. _____.

78. EVALUATION

Meaning:
To determine the importance, effectiveness, or worth of something or situation.

Examples:
1. The *evaluation* of the progress of the students is impossible, unless we have a feedback from their teacher.
2. The *evaluation* of this method may take place only with the help of volunteers who will try it.

To understand more look it up in a dictionary. Then make your own sentences below.

1. _____.
2. _____.
3. _____.

79. INVOICE

Meaning:
An invoice is a detailed list of goods shipped or services rendered, with an account of all costs.

Examples :
1. Do you need an *invoice*? No thanks, just a receipt please.
2. We always ask for a collective *invoice* for office goods each month.

To understand more look it up in a dictionary. Then make your own sentences below.

1. _____.
2. _____.
3. _____.

80. INTEREST RATE

Meaning:
It is the percentage of a sum of money or short-term loans that banks charge or pay their commercial customers.

Examples:
1. High *interest rates* discourage people from taking loans.
2. The best advertisement for a bank is to offer low *interest rates*.

To understand more look it up in a dictionary. Then make your own sentences below.

1. _____.

2. _____.

3. _____.

EXERCISE 7

Choose the best words for the following definitions:

1. Easy to approach, reach, enter, speak with, or use.
   a. Troublesome
   b. Accessible
   c. Mature

2. To put into the mouth and draw upon
   a. To spot
   b. To stroll
   c. To suck

3. Lacking definition; vague or indistinct.
   a. Ordinary
   b. Busy
   c. Indecisive

4. To send from one person, thing, or place to another; convey.
   a. To sneeze
   b. To transmit
   c. To compete

5. Full of distress or affliction.
   a. Troublesome
   b. Challenge
   c. Accessible

6. Suited or favorable to one's comfort, purpose, or needs
   a. Collaborate
   b. Superior
   c. Convenient

7. To work together, especially in a joint intellectual effort.
   a. To Spot
   b. To collaborate
   c. To pronounce

8. Lower someone's spirits; make downhearted
   a. To collaborate
   b. To demoralize
   c. To transmit

9. To announce authoritatively or officially.
   a. To pronounce
   b. To evaluate
   c. To deposit

10. To go for a leisurely walk
    a. To Stroll
    b. To transmit
    c. To collaborate

EXERCISE 8

Choose either (a) or (b) for the following definitions:

1. Different in nature or quality
   a. Distinct
   b. Consult

2. An occupant or inhabitant of any place.
   a. Landlord
   b. Tenant

3. To cause faster or greater activity
   a. To accelerate
   b. To deposit

4. The opposite of landlady
   a. Landlord
   b. Tenant

5. An itemized bill for goods sold or services provided
   a. Interest rate
   b. Invoice

6. Subject to or under the authority of a superior
   a. Subordinate
   b. Superior

7. The opposite of deposit.
   a. To Evaluate
   b. To withdraw

8. Uncertain, hazardous, or risky
   a. Interest rate
   b. Chancy

9. The items represented on a list, as a merchant's stock of goods.
    a. Inventory
    b. Evaluation.

10. The act of pledging, or engaging oneself.
    a. Distinct
    b. Commitment

81. CHANCY

Meaning:
Something is chancy when it is uncertain, hazardous, or risky.

Examples:
1. It was a *chancy* thing to do. You could have died!
2. Building your own home is a *chancy* business.

To understand more look it up in a dictionary. Then make your own sentences below.

1. _____.

2. _____.

3. _____.

82. SUBORDINATE

Meaning::
A Subordinate is in a position of less power or authority than someone else.

Examples:
1. The boss always gives the routine paper work to his *subordinates*.
2. *Subordinates* are often treated badly by their superiors.

To understand more look it up in a dictionary. Then make your own sentences below.

1. _____.

2. _____.

3. _____.

83. INVENTORY

Meaning:
Inventory is a detailed list of articles, giving the code number, quantity, and value of each that are in a place.

Examples:
1. Two new chairs appeared on the *inventory* of our room in the dormitory.
2. Their *inventory* of used computer equipment is the best in the city.

To understand more look it up in a dictionary. Then make your own sentences below.

1. _____.
2. _____.
3. _____.

84. COMMITMENT

Meaning:
Commitment is the state of being emotionally or intellectually devoted, as to a belief, a course of action, or another person.

Examples:
1. He's well known for his *commitment* to right-wing politics.
2. I'm afraid she's got too much *commitment* this month to help you with your project.

To understand more look it up in a dictionary. Then make your own sentences below.

1. _____.
2. _____.
3. _____.

85. APPLICATION

Meaning:
Application is a formal and usually written request for something such as a job, admission to a school, a loan, etc.

Examples:
1. I've sent 10 *applications* for different jobs and haven't received any answer yet.
2. If you want to go to the USA, you'll have to fill in the *application* form for your visa first.

To understand more look it up in a dictionary. Then make your own sentences below.

1. _____.

2. _____.

3. _____.

86. TO MAINTAIN

Meaning:
To maintain is to keep doing something without changing or to keep something in good condition by making repairs, correcting problems.

Examples:
1. The top priority of our company is to *maintain* our high standards.
2. Large buildings are very costly to *maintain.*

To understand more look it up in a dictionary. Then make your own sentences below.

1. _____.

2. _____.

3. _____.

87. MARKET SHARE

Meaning:
This is the percentage that a company has of the total sales for a particular product or service.

Example:
Google's *market share* has recently increased from 10% to 30%.

To understand more look it up in a dictionary. Then make your own sentences below.

1. _____.
2. _____.
3. _____.

88. EXPANSION

Meaning:
Expansion is the act of becoming bigger or of making something bigger.

Examples:
1. There has been rapid *expansion* of the electronics industry as a result of technical development.
2. The multinational companies' *expansion* is one of the reasons for globalization.

To understand more look it up in a dictionary. Then make your own sentences below.

1. _____.
2. _____.
3. _____.

89. TO NEGOTIATE

Meaning:
This word means to discuss something formally in order to make an agreement.

Examples:
1. The government decided to *negotiate* with the nurses on strike.
2. We are *negotiating* a new contract with our overseas customer.

To understand more look it up in a dictionary. Then make your own sentences below.

1. _____.

2. _____.

3. _____.

90. REFERENCES

Meaning:
It is the act of mentioning someone or something or a situation in speech or writing

Examples:
1. With good *references,* you have a big chance of getting your dream job.
2. Young people often start low but after they gain some experience and get *references* from previous employers, they move up and find better jobs.
3. Please, try to avoid making any *reference* to his accident.

To understand more look it up in a dictionary. Then make your own sentences below.

1. _____.

2. _____.

3. _____.

TREASURE BOX 6: MAKE MISTAKES

> Be flexible with the rules of grammar you have learned.
> Do not try to be perfect in a day. Learn from your mistakes.

91. REWARD

Meaning:
A Reward is money or another kind of payment that is given or received or offered for something that has been done or for something that might be done.

Examples:
1. The police has promised a *reward* for revealing the hiding place of the murderer.
2. Our boss often gives *rewards* to employees who contribute to the company's success.

To understand more look it up in a dictionary. Then make your own sentences below.

1. _____.
2. _____.
3. _____.

92. VACANCY

Meaning:
Vacancy is a job or position or room in a hotel, motel, etc. that is available to be taken.

Examples:
1. There are three *vacancies* for shop assistants in the new shopping mall.
2. I wonder if the *vacancy* for a secretary advertised last week is still on.
3. There were no *vacancies* at the hotel

To understand more look it up in a dictionary. Then make your own sentences below.

1. _____.
2. _____.
3. _____.

93. SUPPLEMENT

Meaning:
A supplement is something that is added to something else in order to make it complete.

Examples :
1. The money she earns from translating documents is just a *supplement* to her main income.
2. If you want to use the hotel swimming pool and sauna, you will have to pay a *supplement* to your accommodation.

To understand more look it up in a dictionary. Then make your own sentences below.

1. _____.
2. _____.
3. _____.

94. INCAPABLE

Meaning:
Someone who is incapable of doing something is unable to do it or lacks the ability to do it.

Examples:
1. The company seems *incapable* of protecting itself against the competition.
2. I think she's *incapable* of walking past a clothes shop without buying something.

To understand more look it up in a dictionary. Then make your own sentences below.

1. _____.

2. _____.

3. _____.

95. ESSENTIAL GOODS

Meaning:
A physical item such as food, water, gasoline and shelter required by a consumer in order to sustain health or life is an essential good.

Examples:
1. The cost of *essential goods is* much higher in the west of Europe.
2. People are afraid that joining Euro zone would increase the cost of *essential goods* in Poland.

To understand more look it up in a dictionary. Then make your own sentences below.

1. _____.

2. _____.

3. _____.

96. DEMAND

Meaning:
Demand is the ability and need or desire to buy goods and services

Examples:
1. There's little **demand** for luxury goods in this poor area.
2. Good engineers are always in great **demand.**

To understand more look it up in a dictionary. Then make your own sentences below.

1. _____.
2. _____.
3. _____.

97. SALES REPRESENTATIVE

Meaning:
A sales representative is a person who sells products and services on behalf of a company, usually traveling away from their own company's premises to find and sell to customers.

Examples:
1. People are fed up with numerous calls from **sales representatives** trying to sell them something they don't really need.
2. He makes good impression and is really persuasive, as a great **sales representative**.

To understand more look it up in a dictionary. Then make your own sentences below.

1. _____.
2. _____.
3. _____.

98. REVENUE

Meaning:
Revenue is money that is made by or paid to a business or an organization.

Examples:
1. Companies' *revenues* have fallen considerably at the time of the economic crisis.
2. Taxes that we pay are most of the government's *revenue*.

To understand more look it up in a dictionary. Then make your own sentences below.

1. _____.
2. _____.
3. _____.

99. PERFORMANCE

Meaning:
Performance is the act of doing something such as your job or how well it is done.

Examples:
1. Our employees are given rewards based on their *performance* at work.
2. Experience generally improves *performance*.

To understand more look it up in a dictionary. Then make your own sentences below.

1. _____.
2. _____.
3. _____.

100. SUPPLIER

Meaning:
A Supplier is a person or company or country that provides goods or services.

Examples:
1. AT&T is a leading *supplier* of mobile telephone services in the United States.
2. The building company signed an agreement with the new *supplier* of building materials.

To understand more look it up in a dictionary. Then make your own sentences below.

1. _____.

2. _____.

3. _____.

EXERCISE 9

Choose either (a) or (b) for the following definitions:

1. An increase, enlargement, or development, especially in the activities of a company.
   a. Accelerate
   b. Expansion

2. The specific percentage of total industry sales of a particular product achieved.
   a. Market share
   b. Interest rate

3. To arrange for or bring about by discussion and settlement of terms.
   a. To evaluate
   b. To negotiate

4. A verbal or written request, as for a job, etc
   a. Application
   b. Commitment

5. To keep in a specified, condition, state, position, etc.
   a. To transmit
   b. To maintain

6. The act of mentioning someone or something or a situation in speech or writing.
   a. reference
   b. maintain

7. when something is uncertain, hazardous, or risky.
   a. commitment
   b. chancy

8. A position of less power or authority than someone else.
   a. Subordinate
   b. reference

9. A detailed list of articles, giving the code number, quantity, and value of each.
   a. reference
   b. inventory

10. The state of being emotionally or intellectually devoted.
    a. commitment
    b. transmit

EXERCISE 10

Choose the either a or b that matches the following definitions;

1. A position, office, or place of accommodation that is unfilled or unoccupied
   a. Vacancy
   b. Application

2. Something given or received in recompense for worthy behavior
   a. Expansion
   b. Reward

3. Something added to complete a thing, make up for a deficiency
   a. Negotiate
   b. Supplement

4. Unable to perform adequately; incompetent
   a. Incapable
   b. Expansion

5. A statement about a person's qualifications, character, and dependability
   a. Application
   b. References

6. To require or need as just, urgent, etc.
   a. Demand
   b. Negotiate

7. The collective items or amounts of income of a person, a state, etc.
   a. Essential goods
   b. Revenue

8. A person or organization designated by a company to solicit business on its behalf in a specified territory or foreign country.
   a. Sales representative
   b. Essential goods

9. The execution or accomplishment of work, acts, feats, etc.
   a. Performance
   b. Demand

10. Basic goods or products necessary for everyday life.
    a. Essential goods
    b. performance

EXERCISE 11

Choose a or b word that matches the following definitions;

1. To require or need as just, urgent, etc.
   a. Demand
   b. Negotiate

2. The collective items or amounts of income of a person, a state, etc.
   a. Essential goods
   b. Revenue

3. A person or organization designated by a company to solicit business on its behalf in a specified territory or foreign country.
   a. Sales representative
   b. Essential goods

4. The execution or accomplishment of work, acts, feats, etc.
   a. Performance
   b. Demand

5. Basic goods or products necessary for everyday life.
   a. Essential goods
   b. Performance

101. PARTNERS

Meanings and examples:
1. Someone's husband or wife or the person someone has relationship with.
   * His *partner,* his wife of 20 years, was shocked to hear about his accident.
2. One of two or more people, businesses, etc., that work together or do business together
   * They are *partners* in the real estate business.
   * Singapore's most important trading *partner* is Indonesia.
3. Someone who participates in an activity or game with another person
   * We were each assigned a *partner* for the project.

To understand more look it up in a dictionary. Then make your own sentences below.

1. _____.

2. _____.

3. _____.

102. PARTNERSHIP

Meaning:
It is the state of being partners **or** a relationship between partners

Examples:
1. Partners of a *partnership* have greater liability for the possible losses than shareholders of a corporation.
2. We both used to run our own separate business activities, but last year we established *partnership*.
3. Their marriage is a *partnership* that has remained strong despite family illnesses.

To understand more look it up in a dictionary. Then make your own sentences below.

1. _____.

2. _____.

3. _____.

103. DONATE

Meaning:
To donate is to give money, food, clothes, etc. in order to help a person or organization.

Examples:
1. Some anonymous group of businessmen *donated* a huge amount of money to the charity.
2. Nowadays, many companies *donate* money to environmental protection to create the image of environment-friendly businesses.

To understand more look it up in a dictionary. Then make your own sentences below.

1. _____.

2. _____.

3. _____.

104. SAFETY

Meaning: As noun it means free from danger or risk of injury.
It can also be used as an adjective when describing a characteristic of something which provides safety.

Examples:
1. It's important to learn about *safety* before using power tools.
2. He always wore *safety* glasses when working with chemicals.

To understand more look it up in a dictionary. Then make your own sentences below.

1. _____.

2. _____.

3. _____.

105. HAMMER

Meaning:

A Hammer is a tool with a heavy metal top attached to a straight handle, used for hitting an object such as a nail into a substance that holds it firmly in place.

It also means to repeat again and again.

Examples:

1. "John, please get me my new *hammer* to nail these pieces of wood together."
2. The sound of the rain *hammering* the metal roof of our camper made sleeping nearly impossible.

To understand more look it up in a dictionary. Then make your own sentences below.

1. _____.

2. _____.

3. _____.

TREASURE BOX 7: COOK YOUR ENGLISH.

Yes you read it right, just like a chef, cook your own English, say it the way you feel it, make mistakes and learn.

106. IMPLEMENT

Meaning:
To implement means to put a plan or system into operation.

Examples:
1. The new regulations will be *implemented* next month.
2. The government has finally *implemented* the promised changes to the taxation of income.

To understand more look it up in a dictionary. Then make your own sentences below.

1. _____.

2. _____.

3. _____.

107. FACE

Meaning:
Face means the front of and object or the head including the eyes, nose, and mouth or to deal with a difficult situation.

Examples:
1. she looked so beautiful at her wedding, her *face* glowed with happiness.
2. You need to *face* your difficulties rather than to run away from them.

To understand more look it up in a dictionary. Then make your own sentences below.

1. _____.

2. _____.

3. _____.

108. EAGER

Meaning:
To be eager is to be having or showing desire or interest in doing something.

Examples:
1. She had heard so much about the new school, she was very *eager* to start.
2. He was *eager* to show his wife the gift he had bought her.

To understand more look it up in a dictionary. Then make your own sentences below.

1. _____.
2. _____.
3. _____.

109. EAGLE

Meaning:
An Eagle is a large, strong bird with a curved beak that eats meat and has good sight

Examples:
1. It is amazing how far an *eagle* can see.
2. We both love birds, but the *eagle* is my husband's favorite.

To understand more look it up in a dictionary. Then make your own sentences below.

1. _____.
2. _____.
3. _____.

110. LOAFER

Meaning:
It is a type of shoe with stitches around the top and without shoelaces.
It also means a person who does not work hard.

Examples:
1. He saved up his lawn-mowing money all summer to buy a pair of *loafers.*
2. I guess the boy turned out to be a *loafer* because his father was such a lazy guy.

To understand more look it up in a dictionary. Then make your own sentences below.

1. _____.
2. _____.
3. _____.

111. GROCERY

Meaning:
A grocery a store that sells food and household supplies.

Examples :
1. One of her favorite ways to spend the afternoon was shopping for *groceries.*
2. She has to eat something before she goes to the *grocery store,* or she will buy too much food!

To understand more look it up in a dictionary. Then make your own sentences below.

1. _____.
2. _____.
3. _____.

112. MOBILITY

Meaning:
It means the ability or tendency to move from one position or situation to another quickly and easily.

Examples:
1. People with families don't normally take up this job, because it involves permanent *mobility*.
2. Some young people just cannot stay in one place too long. They often find jobs that require high *mobility*.

To understand more look it up in a dictionary. Then make your own sentences below.

1. _____.
2. _____.
3. _____.

113. TO REMIND

Meaning:
This word means to make someone aware of something forgotten or possibly forgotten, or to bring back a memory to someone.

Examples:
1. *Remind* me to call Sue in the evening, will you?
2. I was enjoying myself at the party, when she had to *remind* me that I must get up early to work. So I left and went home angry.

To understand more look it up in a dictionary. Then make your own sentences below.

1. _____.
2. _____.
3. _____.

114. TRAFFIC JAM

Meaning:
This is a situation of too many vehicles on a road so that they can move only very slowly or not at all.

Examples:
1. I was late again, because I was stuck in a huge *traffic jam* for an hour. I shouldn't have gone by car during rush hours.
2. The main road in the center of the town has been closed recently causing terrible *traffic jams.*

To understand more look it up in a dictionary. Then make your own sentences below.

1. _____.

2. _____.

3. _____.

115. FORECAST

Meaning:
A Forecast is a statement of what is likely to happen in the future.

Examples:
1. The experts *forecast* a huge rise in unemployment due to the economic crisis.
2. A lot of snow has been *forecast* for the following week.

To understand more look it up in a dictionary. Then make your own sentences below.

1. _____.

2. _____.

3. _____.

116. DURING

Meaning:
During means at some time between the beginning and the end of an event.

Examples:
1. The restaurant is open *during* the day.
2. The period *during* which he grew to adulthood.

To understand more look it up in a dictionary. Then make your own sentences below.

1. _____.
2. _____.
3. _____.

117. WHILE

Meaning:
While means a short period of time marked by the occurrence of an action or a condition.

Examples:
1. *While* she appreciated the honor, she could not accept the position.
2. I stay inside *while* it's raining.

To understand more look it up in a dictionary. Then make your own sentences below.

1. _____.
2. _____.
3. _____.

118. LAKE

Meaning:
A Lake is a large area of water that is not salty and is surrounded by land.

Examples:
1. The *Lake* District, a rural area in North West England, is famous for its beautiful lakes surrounded by mountains.
2. We took a boat to cross the *lake*, whereas the others swam across it.

To understand more look it up in a dictionary. Then make your own sentences below.

1. _____.
2. _____.
3. _____.

119. TO HAPPEN

Meaning:
If a situation or event *happens* to someone or something, it has an effect on that person or thing and it is not planned.

Examples:
1. What will *happen* if your parents find out that you're here?
2. What *happened* to you? You look terrible!

To understand more look it up in a dictionary. Then make your own sentences below.

1. _____.
2. _____.
3. _____.

120. TO OFFER

Meaning:
This word means to ask someone if he or she would like to have something or would like you to do something.

Examples:
1. Can I *offer* you a drink?
2. He *offered* that we go to the cinema tonight, but I refused.

To understand more look it up in a dictionary. Then make your own sentences below.

1. _____.

2. _____.

3. _____.

TREASURE BOX 8: USE THESE WORDS

Remember that if you don't use these words regularly, you'll forget them in a very short time. So please use them as much as possible. The more you speak the better you become

EXERCISE 12

Use the following words to fill in the gaps;

DONATE, SAFETY, HAMMER, PARTNERSHIP, SUPPLIER

A big ....of essential goods have formed...................... with some

smaller ones to..................goods and money to help the people affected in the

recent earthquake and tsunami. They especially demanded a quicker steps to make

sure that there is enough provision of...................... environment for all.

They also .... on the quick control of the nuclear radiation and better alternative energy provision in the nearest future.

EXERCISE 13

Fill in the gaps with the following words.

IMPLEMENT, FACE, EAGER, EAGLE, LOAF, GROCERY

1. "What this generation must do is....................... its problems" (John F. Kennedy).

2. He is disliked by almost everyone because he is a ....

3. The government have decided to .... the new procedures.

4. She was very .... to go back to school.

5. Like all birds of prey, ... have very large hooked beaks for tearing flesh from their preys` strong muscular legs, and powerful talons.

6. Cities everywhere are banning plastic .... bags, while one lonely California lawyer fights for their survival.

Exercise 14

Choose the best word that fits each definition.

REMIND, FORECAST, WHILE, MOBILITY, TRAFFIC JAM, DURING

1. The ability to move or be moved freely and easily.

2. In spite of the fact that or at the same time that something else is happening.

3. A number of vehicles so obstructed that they can scarcely move.

4. To contrive or plan beforehand or prearrange or predict.

5. Throughout the course or duration of.

6. To assist (somebody acting or reciting) by suggesting the next words or something forgotten or imperfectly learned.

121. RESPONSIBLE

Meaning:
Responsible means having good judgment and the ability to act correctly and make good decisions.

Examples:
1. I'm not afraid of lending him money or my car, because he's a very *responsible* person.
2. We're looking for a *responsible* babysitter to look after our daughter.

To understand more look it up in a dictionary. Then make your own sentences below.

1. _____.
2. _____.
3. _____.

122. LIBRARY

Meaning:
A Library is a place where books, magazines, and other materials such as videos and musical recordings are available for people to use or borrow

Examples:
1. Ordinary students don't have money to buy new books, so they borrow them from a *library*.
2. When I'm bored, I go to the local *library* to borrow something interesting to read

To understand more look it up in a dictionary. Then make your own sentences below.

1. _____.
2. _____.
3. _____.

123. UNIT

Meaning:
A Unit is a single thing, person, or group that is a part of something larger.

Examples:
1. The standard *unit* of currency in Germany is the euro.
2. The book is divided into 12 *units*, each focused on different area of English grammar.

To understand more look it up in a dictionary. Then make your own sentences below.

1. _____.

2. _____.

3. _____.

124. SUNRISE

Meaning:
Sunrise is the time in the morning when you first see the sun.

Examples:
1. She finished studying for her exam at *sunrise*.
2. We set off early at *sunrise*.

To understand more look it up in a dictionary. Then make your own sentences below.

1. _____.

2. _____.

3. _____.

125. TO PUSH

Meaning:
To push is to cause something to move forward or away from you.

Examples:
1. He *pushed* her into the water, as he didn't know that she can't swim.
2. They *pushed* the door open and went in making all the people look at them.

To understand more look it up in a dictionary. Then make your own sentences below.

1. _____.
2. _____.
3. _____.

126. TO HURT

Meaning:
To hurt is to feel pain, or to cause pain or difficulty or injury to yourself or someone else.

Examples:
1. He *hurt* his leg when he fell from the tree.
2. She *hurt* him so much, when she left without a word of explanation.

To understand more look it up in a dictionary. Then make your own sentences below.

1. _____.
2. _____.
3. _____.

127. LAW

Meaning:
A Law is a rule or a set of rules made by a government that states how people may and may not behave in society and in business, and that often orders particular punishments if they do not obey.

Examples:
1. You can't drink alcohol in the street according to the *law*.
2. They imposed a *law* that forbids smoking in restaurants.

To understand more look it up in a dictionary. Then make your own sentences below.

1. _____.

2. _____.

3. _____.

128. FACTORY

Meaning:
A Factory is a building or buildings where people use machines to produce goods.

Examples:
1. We visited the sweets *factory* and we had our stomachs full of chocolate.
2. Nobody wants to live here because it's an area of *factories*, full of noise and smoke.

To understand more look it up in a dictionary. Then make your own sentences below.

1. _____.

2. _____.

3. _____.

129. ENVIRONMENT

Meaning:
The conditions that you live or work in and the way that they influence how you feel or how effectively you can work is an environment.

Examples:
1. Our natural *environment* is regularly threatened by oil spills and pollution.
2. If you sort out rubbish, you help the *environment*.

To understand more look it up in a dictionary. Then make your own sentences below.

1. _____.
2. _____.
3. _____.

130. DAWN

Meaning:
This is the period in the day when light from the sun begins to appear in the sky.

Examples:
1. People from villages wake up at *dawn* and start working. I can't imagine living like that. I'd rather sleep until midday.
2. When I was a child, I used to wake up at *dawn* and watch the sun rising.

To understand more look it up in a dictionary. Then make your own sentences below.

1. _____.
2. _____.
3. _____.

131. TO DISCUSS

Meaning:
To discuss is to talk about something to other people, often exchanging ideas or opinions.

Examples:
1. We are meeting today to *discuss* our problems.
2. The book *discusses* English literature.

To understand more look it up in a dictionary. Then make your own sentences below.

1. _____.

2. _____.

3. _____.

132. TO RECOGNIZE / RECOGNISE

Meaning:
This word means to know and remember someone or something because of previous knowledge or experience.

Examples:
1. Have you seen Helen recently? She looks so different that I hardly *recognized* her!
2. This is the castle that we visited ten years ago when you were a child. Do you *recognize* it?

To understand more look it up in a dictionary. Then make your own sentences below.

1. _____.

2. _____.

3. _____.

133. FOREIGN

Meaning:
Something can be described as foreign when it is coming from or belonging to a different place or country.

Examples:
1. He can speak two *foreign* languages: English and French.
2. Remember to take your passport. The tour goes through four *foreign* countries.

To understand more look it up in a dictionary. Then make your own sentences below.

1. _____.
2. _____.
3. _____.

134. CURRENTLY

Meaning:
Currently means at the present time or happening or existing now.

Examples:
1. All the options are *currently* available. You can choose whatever you want.
2. Your question is *currently* being discussed. You will get an answer in a short time.

To understand more look it up in a dictionary. Then make your own sentences below.

1. _____.
2. _____.
3. _____.

135. JOBLESS

Meaning:
The jobless means people who do not have jobs.

Examples:
1. The *jobless* may be given unemployment benefits for no longer than 12 months.
2. She often threatens his husband who is currently *jobless* to leave him, unless he finds a job. He seems not to care.

To understand more look it up in a dictionary. Then make your own sentences below.

1. _____.
2. _____.
3. _____.

TREASURE BOX 9: BE LOUD!

What you may consider loud (especially in Japanese society) is just right for English language for people to hear and possibly understand you.

136. BRIBE

Meaning:
A bribe is something valuable such as money that is given to someone often illegally in order to get that person to do something you want.

Examples:
1. Our last boss was convicted for 5 years' imprisonment for accepting **bribes**.
2. Doctors are believed to take **bribes** from drug companies.

To understand more look it up in a dictionary. Then make your own sentences below.

1. _____.
2. _____.
3. _____.

137. REFRAIN

Meanings:
Refrain means to stop yourself from doing something that you want to do. It may also means a phrase or verse that is repeated regularly in a poem or song.

Examples:
1. I usually **refrain** from singing in public, but when I do, I always sing the **refrain**.
2. I was going to make a joke but I **refrained** myself from doing so.

To understand more look it up in a dictionary. Then make your own sentences below.

1. _____.
2. _____.
3. _____.

138. BORROWER / DEBTOR

Meaning:
These words refer to someone who borrows money from a bank or another person or someone who owes money.

Examples:
1. The *debtor* is obliged to pay their financial obligation at the time mentioned in the agreement.
2. The *borrowers* shall provide the history of financial statements and the information on their incomes, if they want to take the loan.

To understand more look it up in a dictionary. Then make your own sentences below.

1. _____.

2. _____.

3. _____.

139. POLITE

Meaning:
This word means behaving in a way that is socially correct and shows respect for other people's feelings.

Examples:
1. I know you don't like them, but you should be more *polite* to them anyway.
2. Teachers complain that there are no **polite** pupils nowadays.

To understand more look it up in a dictionary. Then make your own sentences below.

1. _____.

2. _____.

3. _____.

140. TICKET

Meaning:

A Ticket is a piece of paper that allows you to see a show, participate in an event, travel on a vehicle, etc.

Examples:

1. If you want to see the latest play in the theatre, you need to buy the *tickets* in advance. The play is very popular.
2. I'm sorry, you don't have a *ticket*, Sir. You cannot be allowed to get on board.

To understand more look it up in a dictionary. Then make your own sentences below.

1. _____.

2. _____.

3. _____.

EXERCISE 15

Use the correct form of the following words to fill in the gaps.

LAKE, HAPPEN, OFFER, RESPONSIBLE, UNIT, LIBRARY.

1. The situation .... us the opportunity to learn more.

2. The cabinet is .... to the parliament.

3. There is a .... of spilled coffee on my desk

4. If anything .... to me it'll be your fault.

5. Degree centigrade is **a** .... **of measurement for temperature.**

6. A .... is a place in which literary and artistic materials, such as books, periodicals, newspapers can be borrowed.

EXERCISE 16

Fill in the gaps with correct form of the following words.

SUNRISE, PUSH, LAW, HURT, ENVIRONMENT, FACTORY.

1. The author .... her latest book by making appearances in bookstores.

2. All citizens are equal before the ....

3. The scandal .... the candidate's chances for victory.

4. We shall never understand the natural .... until we see it as a living organism

5. Assembly line is a mechanical system in a .... whereby an article is conveyed through sites at which successive operations are performed on it.

6. We worked from .... to sunset.

EXERCISE 17

Fill in the gaps with an appropriate form of the following words;

DAWN, DISCUSS, RECOGNIZE, FOREIGN, CURRENTLY, JOBLESS.

1. That doesn't sound related, it sounds.........................to the present discussion.

2. Many of the ....moved to town is causing more competition.

3. She is .... working as a lab technician.

4. The union leaders are meeting to..............................about the fate of the factory.

5. They had decided to leave at..............................to be able to make their appointment.

6. The club's president .... the new member.

141. WARRANTY (GUARANTEE)

Meanings:

A Warranty or Guaranty is a written promise by a company the good condition of a product and to repair or replace the product that breaks within a fixed period of time or do again a piece of work that is not satisfactory.

Examples:

1. The computer's on a 2-year *warranty*. Unfortunately, it broke down after the warranty had run off.
2. There are manufacturers that give you a lifelong *guarantee* for their top-quality products.

To understand more look it up in a dictionary. Then make your own sentences below.

1. _____.

2. _____.

3. _____.

142. PATIENCE

Meaning:

Patience is the ability to remain calm and not become annoyed when dealing with problems or with difficult people or situation.

Examples:

1. I don't have the *patience* to wait in line for hours just to buy a ticket.
2. Investors need to have *patience*. The economy will improve soon.

To understand more look it up in a dictionary. Then make your own sentences below.

1. _____.

2. _____.

3. _____.

143. TV COMMERCIAL

Meaning:
A TV commercial is a paid advertisement on television.

Examples:
1. I don't watch films on TV because of the annoying *TV commercials* every 20 minutes.
2. Billboards and other outdoor advertising have become more popular and cheaper than *TV commercials.*

To understand more look it up in a dictionary. Then make your own sentences below.

1. _____.
2. _____.
3. _____.

144. WARDROBE

Meaning:
A wardrobe is a piece of furniture where clothes are kept or a particular type of clothes that a person owns.

Examples:
1. You buy too many clothes. Your *wardrobe* is too small for it.
2. I decided to change my summer *wardrobe,* because all my clothes are so monotonous

To understand more look it up in a dictionary. Then make your own sentences below.

1. _____.
2. _____.
3. _____.

145. ENORMOUS

Meaning:
Enormous means very great in size or amount.

Examples:
1. Have you ever seen such an *enormous* house? It must have at least 200 rooms.
2. This film was an *enormous* success and earned $ 1.000.000 in one week.

To understand more look it up in a dictionary. Then make your own sentences below.

1. _____.
2. _____.
3. _____.

146. TO SMELL

Meaning:
To smell is the ability to notice or recognize a substance in the air by using the nose.

Examples:
1. The milk is not fresh. Can you *smell* it?
2. He got a cold and couldn't *smell* very well.

To understand more look it up in a dictionary. Then make your own sentences below.

1. _____.
2. _____.
3. _____.

147. PEACE

Meaning:
Peace is a period of freedom from war or violence, especially when people live and work together without violent disagreements.

Examples:
1. All I want is to have some *peace* after the stressful day.
2. Terrorism is a serious problem that threatens world *peace.*

To understand more look it up in a dictionary. Then make your own sentences below.

1. _____.
2. _____.
3. _____.

148. TEAR

Meaning:
Tear is a drop of salty liquid that flows from the eye when it is hurt or as a result of strong emotion, especially unhappiness or pain.

Examples:
1. I saw tears streaming down her face. She was not sad they were *tears* of joy.
2. My mum couldn't hide her *tears* when she saw me in a white wedding dress.

To understand more look it up in a dictionary. Then make your own sentences below.

1. _____.
2. _____.
3. _____.

149. RAINBOW

Meaning:
A rainbow is a curved line of colors that appears in the sky when the sun shines while it is raining

Examples:
1. The *rainbow* is a symbol of the alliance with God.
2. I've never seen such a beautiful *rainbow* with all seven saturated colors extending from the heavy clouds to the ground.

To understand more look it up in a dictionary. Then make your own sentences below.

1. _____.

2. _____.

3. _____.

150. TO HIT

Meaning:
To hit is to move your hand or an object quickly so that it touches someone or something in a forceful or violent way.

Examples:
1. She *hit* the thief hard on the stomach with her bag.
2. The ball *hit* the ground and the match was over.

To understand more look it up in a dictionary. Then make your own sentences below.

1. _____.

2. _____.

3. _____.

TREASURE BOX10: BE CONSISTENT

> One of the secrets of becoming a good English speaker is being consistent. You have to continually learn English if you really want to be fluent at it.

151. PENSION

Meaning:
This is a sum of money paid regularly to a person who has stopped working because of having reached a certain age.

Examples:
1. Older people often find it hard to live on their *pensions* only.
2. I'd like to draw my *pension* much earlier. I'm really fed up with my job.

To understand more look it up in a dictionary. Then make your own sentences below.

1. _____.
2. _____.
3. _____.

152. CRIME

Meaning:
A crime is an illegal act for which someone can be punished by the government.

Examples:
1. He was sentenced to prison for having committed a terrible *crime.*
2. Those who sell drugs commit a serious *crime.*

To understand more look it up in a dictionary. Then make your own sentences below.

1. _____.
2. _____.
3. _____.

153. FOCUS

Meaning:
The word focus means to direct attention toward something or someone.

Examples:
1. We need to *focus* our efforts *on* getting the work done.
2. She has an amazing ability to *focus* for hours at a time.

To understand more look it up in a dictionary. Then make your own sentences below.

1. _____.
2. _____.
3. _____.

154. ATTRACTIVE

Meaning:
Something or someone may be attractive for having a feature or quality that people like.

Examples:
1. An *attractive* woman greeted us at the door.
2. The camera has many **attractive** features at a very *attractive* price.

To understand more look it up in a dictionary. Then make your own sentences below.

1. _____.

2. _____.

3. _____.

155. INCIDENT

Meaning:
An incident is an unexpected and usually unpleasant thing that happens.

Examples:
1. Two people were shot yesterday in two separate *incidents*.
2. Many of such *incidents* go unreported.

To understand more look it up in a dictionary. Then make your own sentences below.

1. _____.

2. _____.

3. _____.

156. AVOID

Meaning:
This word means to stay away from someone or something, or prevent something from happening, or not allow yourself to do something.

Examples:
1. They successfully *avoided* each other for days.
2. We need to *avoid* further delays.

To understand more look it up in a dictionary. Then make your own sentences below.

1. _____.
2. _____.
3. _____.

157. MEANINGFUL

Meaning:
Something or action is meaningful if it has a real importance or value.

Examples:
1. The test did not produce any *meaningful* results.
2. He wanted to feel that his job was *meaningful*.

To understand more look it up in a dictionary. Then make your own sentences below.

1. _____.
2. _____.
3. _____.

158. POTENTIAL

Meaning:
Potential is a chance or possibility that something will happen or exist in the future.

Examples:
1. Doctors are excited about the new drug's *potential* benefits.
2. He is a *potential* candidate for president.

To understand more look it up in a dictionary. Then make your own sentences below.

1. _____.

2. _____.

3. _____.

159. PROMOTE

Meaning:
To promote means to change the rank or position of someone to a higher or more important one or to help something happen, develop, or increase.

Examples:
1. He was *promoted* to senior editor.
2. Good soil *promotes* plant growth.

To understand more look it up in a dictionary. Then make your own sentences below.

1. _____.

2. _____.

3. _____.

160. GRUMBLE

Meaning:
To grumble is to complain quietly about something or to make a low, heavy sound.

Examples:
1. There's been a lot of *grumbling* among the employees.
2. We could hear thunder *grumbling* in the distance.

To understand more look it up in a dictionary. Then make your own sentences below.

1. _____.

2. _____.

3. _____.

EXERCISE 18

Fill in the gaps with the right forms of the following words;

BRIBE, REFRAIN, DEBTOR, POLITE, TICKET, WARRANTY

1. If a creditor has loaned money, performed services or provided a ....
    with a product, that.........has to pay the creditor.

2. You are asked to .... from smoking, drinking(alcohol) and eating
    in this hall.

3. The stereo and the refrigerator came with a three-year ....but one
    year for the TV.

4. We bought .... for the opera I got one for over speeding on the
    way there.

5. She received some .... applause despite the mistakes in her
    performance.

EXERCISE 19

Fill in the gaps with the correct form of the following words.

PATIENCE, WARDROBE, ENORMOUS, SMELL, BRIBE, PEACE, TV COMMERCIAL.

1. We chose not to undertake the project because of the ....costs involved.

2. I can't .... anything because I'm so stuffed up.

3. After many years of war, people on both sides were longing for ....

4. I offered the children a .... for finishing their homework.

5. She has a new summer ....and she almost can't wait for summer to come.

6. The average American sees and hears thousands of .... messages each day.

7. She treated her students with great .... and humor.

EXERCISE 20

Fill in the gaps with the right form of the following words.

TEAR, RAINBOW, PENSION, FOCUS, CRIME, HIT, MAKE, LET

1. They ....off when they found a younger man for the job.

2. There are fairy tales of searches for the pot of gold at the foot of the ....

3. There's no greater .... than forgetting your anniversary.

4. The day's news coverage .... primarily/mainly *on* the scandal.

5. He was in ....over the death of his dog.

6. The teacher ....her students memorize long lists of vocabularies.

7. A break in the cloud ....us see the top of the mountain.

8. The plate shattered when it ....the floor.

EXERCISE 21

Fill in the gaps with the correct form of the following words.

ATTRACTIVE, INCIDENT, AVOID, MEANINGFUL, POTENTIAL, PROMOTE,

1. How can I .... paying too much tax?

2. His ideas are .... *to* many people.

3. The project has .... risks and advantages.

4. The trip turned out to be very .... to both of them.

5. Aside from a few isolated .... the crowd was well-behaved.

6. The Chiba prefecture office distributed pamphlets ....good dental hygiene.

161. PROHIBIT

Meaning:
To prohibit an activity is to prevent it by forbidding it.

Examples:
1. The rules of the company *prohibit* dating a coworker.
2. The prison's electric fence *prohibits* escape of the prisoners.

To understand more look it up in a dictionary. Then make your own sentences below.

1. _____.

2. _____.

3. _____.

162. CAMP

Meaning:
A camp is a place that is usually far away from cities and that has tents, small houses, etc. where people can do different activities especially during the summer.

Examples:
1. The children have fond memories of their last summer *camp*.
2. Our star pitcher injured his arm during the spring *camp* training.

To understand more look it up in a dictionary. Then make your own sentences below.

1. _____.

2. _____.

3. _____.

163. DESTINATION

Meaning:
Destination is the place where someone is going or where something is being sent or taken

Examples:
1. After stopping for lunch, we continued on toward our *destination*.
2. The package arrived its *destination* two days later.

To understand more look it up in a dictionary. Then make your own sentences below.

1. _____.

2. _____.

3. _____.

164. DISEMBARK

Meaning:
To disembark is to leave or remove something or someone from a ship or airplane.

Examples:
1. Several passengers *disembarked* from the plane.
2. We will *disembark* the passengers at Yokohama shore.

To understand more look it up in a dictionary. Then make your own sentences below.

1. _____.

2. _____.

3. _____.

165. EMBARK (EMBARKMENT)

Meaning:
Embarkment is to get on board to begin a journey especially on a ship or airplane or to set out on a venture.

Examples:
1. The troops are waiting to *embark* to IRAQ for a special mission.
2. He *embarked* on a new career because he wanted something more exciting.

To understand more look it up in a dictionary. Then make your own sentences below.

1. _____.

2. _____.

3. _____.

TREASURE BOX 11: EXPLAIN YOUR VOCABULARY.

When you are stuck and you cannot remember the word or vocabulary you want to use, simply explain it then you may remember or the person you are talking to may help you out and/or catch what you intend to say.

166. CRISIS

Meaning:
Crisis is a difficult or dangerous situation that needs serious attention.

Examples:
1. Most people blame the government for the country's worsening economic *crisis.*
2. In times of national *crisis,* we need strong leaders we can trust.

To understand more look it up in a dictionary. Then make your own sentences below.

1. _____.
2. _____.
3. _____.

167. DESTINY

Meaning:
Destiny is the force that some people think controls what happens to someone in the future, and which cannot be influenced by them.

Examples:
1. They believed it was their *destiny* to be together.
2. The factory's closing shaped the *destiny* of the entire town.

To understand more look it up in a dictionary. Then make your own sentences below.

1. _____.
2. _____.
3. _____.

168. GLOBAL

Meaning:
Global means involving the entire world.

Examples:
1. English is becoming a *global* language.
2. The *global* economy has become increasingly unstable.

To understand more look it up in a dictionary. Then make your own sentences below.

1. _____.
2. _____.
3. _____.

169. FATIGUE

Meaning:
Fatigue is the condition of being extremely tired:

Examples:
1. We were overcome by *fatigue* after the long journey.
2. The drug's side effects include headache and *fatigue.*

To understand more look it up in a dictionary. Then make your own sentences below.

1. _____.
2. _____.
3. _____.

170. DEMONSTRATE

Meaning:
The word means to show or explain how something is used or done. It also means to take part in an event in which people gather together in order to show that they support or oppose something or someone

Examples:
1. One of the instructors gave or did a *demonstration* of how to prune a tree.
2. Students took part in several peaceful *demonstrations* against the government.

To understand more look it up in a dictionary. Then make your own sentences below.

1. _____.

2. _____.

3. _____.

171. AGGRESSIVE

Meaning:
Being aggressive is to be ready and willing to fight, argue, or using forceful methods to succeed or to do something.

Examples:
1. He started to get *aggressive* and began to shout.
2. **The city began an *aggressive* campaign to encourage recycling.**

To understand more look it up in a dictionary. Then make your own sentences below.

1. _____.

2. _____.

3. _____.

172. ENCOURAGE

Meaning:
To encourage is to make someone more determined, hopeful, and confident or to give advice to them to do something.

Examples:
1. I am *encouraged* that the project seems to be moving ahead.
2. The program is meant to *encourage* energy savings.

To understand more look it up in a dictionary. Then make your own sentences below.

1. _____.

2. _____.

3. _____.

173. ALTERNATIVE

Meaning:
Alternative is a choice or an option or something that can be chosen instead of something else

Examples:
1. We should have *alternative* plans in case the weather is bad.
2. We could meet at the library or, *alternatively*, we could all meet at my house.

To understand more look it up in a dictionary. Then make your own sentences below.

1. _____.

2. _____.

3. _____.

174. POOR

Meaning:
To be poor is having little money or few possessions or not having the basic things that people need to live properly

Examples :
1. It's a very **poor** country. Hardly can anyone afford a car there.
2. They were too **poor** to afford even a pair of new shoes, whereas their children were living in a luxury.

To understand more look it up in a dictionary. Then make your own sentences below.

1. _____.

2. _____.

3. _____.

175. STRAIGHTFORWARD

Meaning:
Something is straightforward when it is easy to understand or when someone is honest.

Examples:
1. Using the computer program is fairly *straightforward*.
2. She gave a *straightforward* account of what happened.

To understand more look it up in a dictionary. Then make your own sentences below.

1. _____.

2. _____.

3. _____.

176. REMARKABLE

Meaning:
Something is remarkable when it is attracting or worthy of notice, especially for being unusual or extraordinary

Examples:
1. Competing in the Olympics is a *remarkable* achievement.
2. The girl has a *remarkable* talent.

To understand more look it up in a dictionary. Then make your own sentences below.

1. _____.

2. _____.

3. _____.

177. TERMINATE

Meaning:
To terminate is to end or stop, or to cause something to end or stop

Examples:
1. The rail line *terminates* in Boston.
2. His contract was *terminated* last month.

To understand more look it up in a dictionary. Then make your own sentences below.

1. _____.

2. _____.

3. _____.

178. HUMBLE

Meaning:
You are humble when you are not thinking of yourself as better than other people.

Examples:
1. He is very *humble* about his achievements.
2. In my *humble* opinion [=in my opinion], he is the most talented actor on the stage today.

To understand more look it up in a dictionary. Then make your own sentences below.

1. _____.

2. _____.

3. _____.

179. LEGACY

Meaning:
Legacy is something handed down from an ancestor or a predecessor or from the past.

Examples:
1. She left us a *legacy* of a million dollars.
2. The war left a *legacy of* pain and suffering.

To understand more look it up in a dictionary. Then make your own sentences below.

1. _____.

2. _____.

3. _____.

180. RETAIN

Meaning:
To retain something is to keep or continue to have it

Examples:
1. The TV show has *retained* its popularity for many years.
2. The company's goal is to attract and *retain* good employees.

To understand more look it up in a dictionary. Then make your own sentences below.

1. _____.

2. _____.

3. _____.

TREASURE BOX 12: LAUGH AT YOURSELF.

When you make mistakes, laugh and joke about it. Do not worry it's all part of learning.

EXERCISE 22

Match the following definitions with the words below.

GRUMBLE, PROHIBIT, CAMP, DESTNATION, DISEMBARK, EMBARK

1. To go on board a vehicle for transportation.

2. To complain quietly about something or to talk in an unhappy way.

3. A place to which one is journeying or to which something is sent.

4. To start or engage, enlist, or invest in an enterprise.

5. A group of people who support or believe in certain ideas.

6. To prevent or to forbid by authority from doing something.

7. A place where athletes train before the beginning of a season.

8. To get out of a vehicle or craft.

9. A place usually in the mountains or by a lake where young people can do different activities during the summer.

10. To go or to remove ashore out of a ship.

EXERCISE 23

Fill in the gaps with the correct form of the following words.

DESTINY, CRISIS, GLOBAL, FATIGUE, DEMONSTRATE, AGGRESSIVE

1. A year ago, both companies were in ....but revived by government's aid.

2. "I'm so .... of your mother and her complaints about my food"

3. The company took .... steps to prevent illegal use of their equipment.

4. The program allows users to do ....searches through all the available data.

5. They brought some bread to share as a .... of goodwill.

6. Nancy wondered whether it was her ....to live in England and marry Melvyn.

Exercise 24

Match the following definitions with the words below.

ENCOURAGE, ALTERNATE, REMARKABLE, TERMINATE, POOR, STRAIGHTFORWARD

1. lacking a normal or adequate supply of something specified.

2. Easy to do or understand, not complicated, honest and open.

3. To end in a particular way or at a particular place.

4. To make (someone) more determined, hopeful, or confident.

5. Existing or functioning outside of the established society: offering or expressing a choice.

6. Unusual or surprising : likely to be noticed.

181. CONTEXT

Meaning:
Context is the part of a text or statement that surrounds a particular word or passage and determines its meaning.

Examples:
1. To really know a word, you must be able to use it *in context*.
2. The actor claimed he'd been quoted *out of context*.

To understand more look it up in a dictionary. Then make your own sentences below.

1. _____.

2. _____.

3. _____.

182. RALLY

Meaning:
This is a public meeting of a large group of people, especially to show support for a particular opinion, political party, or sports team

Examples:
1. Supporters held a *rally* for the candidate.
2. The team's late-game *rally* (*comeback*) helped them win the game.

To understand more look it up in a dictionary. Then make your own sentences below.

1. _____.

2. _____.

3. _____.

183. FRUSTRATE

Meaning:
This means to prevent someone from accomplishing a purpose or fulfilling a desire.

Examples:
1. It *frustrated* him to miss so many games because of injuries.
2. The lack of investors has *frustrated* them in their efforts to expand the company

To understand more look it up in a dictionary. Then make your own sentences below.

1. _____.

2. _____.

3. _____.

184. TREMENDOUS

Meaning:
Someone or something that is tremendous is extremely good, great in amount, size, or degree.

Examples:
1. He has a *tremendous* amount of energy.
2. We had a *tremendous* time.

To understand more look it up in a dictionary. Then make your own sentences below.

1. _____.

2. _____.

3. _____.

185. COMMENTARY

Meaning:
This is a series of remarks describing an event, especially on radio or television, or a set of written notes explaining or expressing an opinion on a text or subject.

Examples:
1. The magazine includes humor and social *commentary*.
2. He provided *commentary* during the game.

To understand more look it up in a dictionary. Then make your own sentences below.

1. _____.
2. _____.
3. _____.

186. OVERTAKE

Meaning:
It means to go beyond something by being a greater amount or degree, or to come from behind and move in front it.

Examples:
1. She *overtook* the other runners and went on to win the race.
2. The pounding rainstorm *overtook* them just outside the city.

To understand more look it up in a dictionary. Then make your own sentences below.

1. _____.
2. _____.
3. _____.

187. DISPLAY

Meaning:
This word means to show something or a collection of things in an organized way for people to see.

Examples:
1. Students *displayed* their projects at the science fair.
2. He *displayed* no emotion when I told him the news.

To understand more look it up in a dictionary. Then make your own sentences below.

1. _____.
2. _____.
3. _____.

188. MODE

Meaning:
This is a way of operating, living, or behaving.

Examples :
1. We're changing the factory's *mode* (*method*) *of* operation in order to save money.
2. When taking pictures indoors, put the camera in flash *mode*.

To understand more look it up in a dictionary. Then make your own sentences below.

1. _____.
2. _____.
3. _____.

189. HARDSHIP

Meaning:
Hardship is a condition of life that causes ongoing or persistent suffering or difficulty.

Examples:
1. He had suffered through considerable *hardship*.
2. The city has been experiencing a period of financial *hardship*.

To understand more look it up in a dictionary. Then make your own sentences below.

1. _____.

2. _____.

3. _____.

190. NEEDY

Meaning:
This word means to be very poor or in need of affection, attention, or reassurance.

Examples:
1. As a child, she was extremely *needy* and had no self-confidence.
2. Our church collected food for the *needy* last week.

To understand more look it up in a dictionary. Then make your own sentences below.

1. _____.

2. _____.

3. _____.

191. PERSONNEL

Meaning:
It means the people who work for a particular company or organization or a department within a company or organization that deals with the people who work for it.

Examples :
1. They've reduced the number of *personnel* working on the project.
2. Talk to *personnel* if you have any questions about your health insurance.

To understand more look it up in a dictionary. Then make your own sentences below.

1. _____.

2. _____.

3. _____.

192. PROLONG

Meaning:
To prolong is to make something last a longer time.

Examples :
1. Chemotherapy helped to *prolong* [=*extend*] her life.
2. Additives are used to *prolong* the shelf life of packaged food

To understand more look it up in a dictionary. Then make your own sentences below.

1. _____.

2. _____.

3. _____.

193. SOUR

Meaning:
To sour is to become unpleasant in taste or unfriendly in manner or attitude.

Examples :
1. The milk had turned/gone *sour*.
2. Their relationship ended *on a sour note*. (ended unpleasantly).

To understand more look it up in a dictionary. Then make your own sentences below.

1. _____.

2. _____.

3. _____.

194. ASTONISH

Meaning:
This word means to cause a feeling of great wonder or surprise in someone.

Examples :
1. Her easy humor and keen intellect *astonishes* me.
2. The garden *astonishes* (*amazes*) anyone who sees it.

To understand more look it up in a dictionary. Then make your own sentences below.

1. _____.

2. _____.

3. _____.

195. NOSEDIVE

Meaning:
This word means a sudden sharp drop made by an airplane with its front end pointing toward the ground or a sudden sharp drop in price, value, condition, etc.

Examples:
1. The plane went *into a **nosedive***.
2. The stock market took a ***nosedive***.

To understand more look it up in a dictionary. Then make your own sentences below.

1. _____.

2. _____.

3. _____.

TREASURE BOX 13: USE YOUR ENGLISH.

Try to use your English by;

a) Reading out loud.

b) Speaking to yourself in English when you're alone, it helps.

c) Writing journal of your daily activities.

196. FRAGILE

Meaning:
Something is fragile if it can be easily broken or damaged or destroyed.

Examples:
1. He is in an emotionally *fragile* state.
2. The two countries have formed a *fragile* coalition.

To understand more look it up in a dictionary. Then make your own sentences below.

1. _____.

2. _____.

3. _____.

197. CONFISCATE

Meaning:
This means to officially take private property away from someone especially as a penalty for wrongdoing.

Examples:
1. Guards *confiscated* knives and other weapons from the prisoners.
2. The teacher *confiscated* all cell phones for the duration of the field trip.

To understand more look it up in a dictionary. Then make your own sentences below.

1. _____.

2. _____.

3. _____.

198. DISREGARD

Meaning:
This word means to ignore something or treat something as unimportant.

Examples:
1. Please *disregard* what I said before.
2. He *disregarded* his father's advice and left school.

To understand more look it up in a dictionary. Then make your own sentences below.

1. _____.

2. _____.

3. _____.

199. FAMINE

Meaning:
This is a situation in which many people do not have enough food to eat in a region, causing suffering and death.

Examples:
1. The *famine* affected half the country.
2. Millions were killed by war, drought, and *famine*.

To understand more look it up in a dictionary. Then make your own sentences below.

1. _____.

2. _____.

3. _____.

200. Obsess

Meaning:
This word means to think and talk about someone or something too much.

Examples:
1. She became more and more **obsessed** with the project.
2. I'm trying to **obsess** less about my weight.

To understand more look it up in a dictionary. Then make your own sentences below.

1. _____.

2. _____.

3. _____.

EXERCISE 25

Fill the gaps with the correct form of the following words;

HUMBLE, LEGACY, RETAIN, CONTEXT, RALLY, FRUSTRATE.

1. A landlord may .... part of your deposit if you break the lease.

2. She's not ashamed of her .... beginnings.

3. The plans to rebuild Fukushima have been .... by bureaucratic delays.

4. The home team .... in the ninth inning to win the game.

5. The book puts these events in their proper historical and social ....

6. He left his children a .... of love and respect.

EXERCISE 26

Match the following definitions with the appropriate words bellow.

TREMENDOUS, COMMENTARY, OVERTAKE, DISPLAY, MODE, HARDSHIP.

1. A specified way of thinking, feeling, acting or doing something.

2. Very good or excellent, wonderful or very large or great.

3. To put (something) where people can see it or to show that you have (an emotion, quality, skill etc.

4. A spoken description of an event (such as a sports contest) as it is happening.

5. Pain and suffering or something that causes pain, suffering, or loss.

6. To catch up with; draw even or level with or to pass after catching up with.

EXERCISE 27

Fill in the gaps with the following words.

NEEDY, PERSONNEL, PROLONG, SOUR, ASTONISH, NOSEDIVE

1. He was too _____ to speak when he saw the present from his children.

2. The team's victory was _____ by an injury to one of their best players.

3. Generous people regularly give money and donate clothes to help the _____.

4. High interest rates are _____ the economy recession.

5. Everyone screamed as the plane suddenly went into a _____.

6. They've reduced the number of _____ working on the project.

EXERCISE 28

Choose the best word for the following definitions.

1. Possible to be easily broken or damaged.
    a. Fever
    b. To notice
    c. Fragile

2. To seize temporarily or permanently as way of penalty for use.
    a. Technique
    b. Confiscate
    c. To notice

3. To ignore (something) or treat (something) as unimportant.
    a. Compliment
    b. Disregard
    c. To recommend

4. A situation in which many people do not have enough food to eat.
    a. Famine
    b. Stranger
    c. Economy

5. To think about something unceasingly or persistently.
    a. Rich
    b. Recommend
    c. Obsess

201. REMOTE

Meaning:
Remote means far away in distance, time, houses, cities, other people.
It may also means very small.

Examples:
1. The mission is to transport medical supplies to *remote* areas of the globe.
2. There is a *remote* possibility that I'll be free Friday night.

To understand more look it up in a dictionary. Then make your own sentences below.

1. _____.

2. _____.

3. _____.

202. INVOLVE

Meaning:
The word means to cause someone or something to be included in some activity, situation or to take part in something

Examples:
1. She remained **involved** with the organization for many years.
2. Renovating the house *involved* hiring a contractor.

To understand more look it up in a dictionary. Then make your own sentences below.

1. _____.

2. _____.

3. _____.

203. FACILITATE

Meaning:
To facilitate a process, something or situation is to make it possible or easier.

Examples:
1. Cutting taxes may *facilitate* economic recovery.
2. Her rise to power was *facilitated* by her influential friends.

To understand more look it up in a dictionary. Then make your own sentences below.

1. _____.

2. _____.

3. _____.

204. TO OBSTRUCT

Meaning:
To obstruct is to slow down, get in the way or block the movement, progress, or action of something or someone.

Examples:
1. A large tree *obstructed* the road
2. She was charged with *obstructing* police.

Try to find the meaning of this word and more uses in the dictionary.

To understand more look it up in a dictionary. Then make your own sentences below.

1. _____.

2. _____.

3. _____.

205. PROFICIENT

Meaning:
This word means to be very good at doing something.

Examples:
1. He has become very *proficient* at computer programming.
2. She is *proficient* in two foreign languages.

To understand more look it up in a dictionary. Then make your own sentences below.

1. _____.

2. _____.

3. _____.

206. OBSTINATE

Meaning:
This word means to be unwilling to change your opinion or action despite persuasion.

Examples:
1. Terrorism is a very *obstinate* problem facing the world.
2. My parents remain as *obstinate* as ever toward possible relocation.

To understand more look it up in a dictionary. Then make your own sentences below.

1. _____.

2. _____.

3. _____.

207. OBSTACLE

Meaning:
Something that stands in the way or that blocks you so that movement, going forward, or progress is prevented.

Examples:
1. He overcame the **obstacles** of poverty and neglect.
2. They must overcome a number of **obstacles** before the restaurant can be opened.

To understand more look it up in a dictionary. Then make your own sentences below.

1. _____.
2. _____.
3. _____.

208. IMPRESS

Meaning:
If you impress something on someone, you cause them to understand its importance.
If you impress someone, you cause them to feel admiration or interest.

Examples:
1. I am **impressed** that you can play the violin so well.
2. The speaker tried to **impress** the dangers of drugs *on* the children.
3. A design was **impressed** on the book's cover.

To understand more look it up in a dictionary. Then make your own sentences below.

1. _____.
2. _____.
3. _____.

209. OUTBREAK

Meaning:
This is a sudden appearance of something such as disease or something else dangerous or unpleasant.

Examples :
1. There was an *outbreak* of violence and war in the northern part of Africa.
2. They are preparing for an *outbreak* of the virus.

To understand more look it up in a dictionary. Then make your own sentences below.

1. _____.
2. _____.
3. _____.

210. TO BOOST

Meaning:
To boost is to improve, motivate or increase something, situation or action.

Examples:
1. The company needs to find ways to *boost* their staff's morale.
2. She *boosted* the boy onto his father's shoulders.

To understand more look it up in a dictionary. Then make your own sentences below.

1. _____.
2. _____.
3. _____.

TREASURE BOX 14: GESTURE!

Gesture a lot with your head, face, hands and even your whole body when you speak. People will find you interesting and want to understand and **connect** with you by all means.

211. ABSTRACT

Meaning:
This means existing as an idea, feeling, or quality, not concrete or not as a material object.
It may also means to take away or remove from a source.

Examples:
1. Data for the study was *abstracted* from hospital records.
2. Personal problems *abstracted* him so persistently.

To understand more look it up in a dictionary. Then make your own sentences below.

1. _____.

2. _____.

3. _____.

212. ELIGIBLE

Meaning:
This word means qualified to do something or be chosen to take part in an activity.

Examples:
1. I'd like to vote but I'm not *eligible* yet.
2. He won't be *eligible* to retire until next year.

To understand more look it up in a dictionary. Then make your own sentences below.

1. _____.
2. _____.
3. _____.

213. REPLY

Meaning:
To reply is to say, write, or do something as an answer or response to a question.

Examples:
1. I called out to them, but no one *replied*.
2. He *replied* politely that he felt a little better.

To understand more look it up in a dictionary. Then make your own sentences below.

1. _____.
2. _____.
3. _____.

214. LEARN THE ROPES

Meaning:
If you learn the ropes, you learn how to do a job properly, or how to get things done.

Examples:
1. Karen will teach you what to do, and it shouldn't take you too long to *learn the ropes*.
2. It can take quite a while for a new lawyer to *learn the ropes* in a big legal firm.

To understand more look it up in a dictionary. Then make your own sentences below.

1. _____.

2. _____.

3. _____.

215. TO EXCLAIM

Meaning:
To exclaim is to say or shout something suddenly because of surprise, pleasure or anger.

Examples:
1. She *exclaimed* in delight over the Christmas tree.
2. The children *exclaimed* with wonder when they saw the elephant.

To understand more look it up in a dictionary. Then make your own sentences below.

1. _____.

2. _____.

3. _____.

216. FOUND

Meaning:
Found (past of Find) is to come upon or discover by searching or making an effort.

Examples:
1. The well diggers *found* a number of Native American artifacts.
2. After an hour of searching, I finally *found* my glasses

To understand more look it up in a dictionary. Then make your own sentences below.

1. _____.
2. _____.
3. _____.

217. BEGGAR

Meaning:
A beggar is a poor person who lives by asking others for money or food.

Examples:
1. He's a lazy *beggar*.
2. Pitiful *beggars* are such a common sight in underdeveloped countries.

To understand more look it up in a dictionary. Then make your own sentences below.

1. _____.
2. _____.
3. _____.

218. REPLACE

Meaning:
To replace is to change for or to take the place of something or put in the place of something or someone else

Examples:
1. Will computers ever completely *replace* books?
2. She was hired to *replace* the previous manager.

To understand more look it up in a dictionary. Then make your own sentences below.

1. _____.

2. _____.

3. _____.

219. DIMENSION

Meaning:
It is a measurement of something in a particular direction, especially its height, length, or width.

Examples:
1. She carefully measured each *dimension* of the room.
2. Please, do not underestimated the *dimensions* of this problem.

To understand more look it up in a dictionary. Then make your own sentences below.

1. _____.

2. _____.

3. _____.

220. CONTRAST

Meaning:
This means to compare two people or things in order to show the differences between them or an obvious difference between two or more things.

Examples:
1. Her black dress *contrasts* sharply *with* the white background.
2. We compared and *contrasted* the two characters of the story.

To understand more look it up in a dictionary. Then make your own sentences below.

1. _____.

2. _____.

3. _____.

EXERCISE 29

Fill in the gaps with the correct form of the following words;

REMOTE, INVOLVE, FACILITATE, OBSTRUCT, PROFICIENT, OBSTINATE

1. He told us a story _____ life on a farm.

2. A piece of food _____ his airway and caused him to stop breathing.

3. She became very _____ in her old age.

4. The moderator's role is to _____ the discussion by asking appropriate questions.

5. He is an _____ child with a violent temper.

6. He shows a high level of _____ in Spanish.

EXERCISE 30

Fill in the space with the appropriate form of the following words.

OBSTACLE, IMPRESS, OUTBREAK, BOOST, ABSTRACT, ELIGIBLE

1. There was an immediate -------------- of paper shuffling and a pretense of work when the supervisor passed through the room.

2. Honesty, truth and justice are ------------- words.

3. The are working hard to ---------- the value of money on their children.

4. It has been more than six years since the fall of the Taliban, fewer than 30% girls are -----------to enroll in schools.

5. Lack of experience is a major ------------- for her opponent.

6. The article discusses a number of ways people can-------- their immune systems.

EXERCISE 31

The doorbell rang, and the housewife answered it. She found two beggars outside. "So, you're begging in twos now?!" she exclaimed. "No, only for today," one of them replied. "I'm showing my replacement the ropes before going on holiday."

Make the best choice.

1. A 'beggar' is a person who.......
   a. Sells food and clothes
   b. has no money
   c. asks for money
   d. does the housework

2. To 'exclaim' means to..........
   a. say something kindly
   b. say suddenly and loudly
   c. walk quickly
   d. look angrily

3. A .... is a person that you put in place of yourself or another.
   a. beggar
   b. rope
   c. housewife
   d. replacement

4. 'Ropes' here means ....
   a. the rules and customs in a place or activity
   b. pieces of strong thick cord
   c. people you probably meet in a special place
   d. houses which are expensive

5. 'Reply' means.....................
   a. to take someone for a ride
   b. to ignore someone
   c. to respond in words or writing
   d. to make a loud noise

6. 'found' here means
   a. to invent something
   b. to gain or regain the use or power of something
   c. to be determined
   d. to come upon or see often accidentally

221. To Infect

Meaning:
This means to cause disease in someone by introducing organisms such as bacteria or viruses. It may also mean to cause someone to feel an emotion.

Examples:
1. If you're sick you should stay home to avoid *infecting* other people in the office.
2. Her enthusiasm has *infected* everyone.

To understand more look it up in a dictionary. Then make your own sentences below.

1. _____.
2. _____.
3. _____.

222. Legible

Meaning:
A writing or print is legible when it is capable of being read easily.

Examples:
1. She has a *legible* handwriting.
2. The document is not *legible*.

To understand more look it up in a dictionary. Then make your own sentences below.

1. _____.
2. _____.
3. _____.

223. SUSPECT

Meaning:
This means to think that something possibly exists, is true, will happen. It may also means to think that someone is possibly guilty of doing something wrong.

Examples:
1. He's *suspected* of involving in four burglaries.
2. Call the doctor immediately if you *suspect* you've been infected.

To understand more look it up in a dictionary. Then make your own sentences below.

1. _____.
2. _____.
3. _____.

224. TRAUMA

Meaning:
It is a very difficult or unpleasant experience that causes someone to have mental or emotional problems usually for a long time.

Examples :
1. She never fully recovered from the *trauma* of her experiences.
2. The accident victim sustained multiple *traumas*.

To understand more look it up in a dictionary. Then make your own sentences below.

1. _____.
2. _____.
3. _____.

225. KNOB

Meaning:
It is a round handle or a small, round device for controlling a machine or electrical equipment.

Examples :
1. The left **knob** controls the volume.
2. The **knob** (doorknob) is stuck and I can't open the door!

To understand more look it up in a dictionary. Then make your own sentences below.

1. _____.

2. _____.

3. _____.

TREASURE BOX 15: TALK TO YOURSELF IN ENGLISH

You can also practice *speaking to yourself* in English, but be careful! Do this in your house or in your head, not when you are in the midst of people.

226. AWARE

Meaning:
This means knowing that something exists, or having knowledge or experience of a particular thing.

Examples:
1. I was not fully *aware* of the danger.
2. Students today are very *aware* about the environment.

To understand more look it up in a dictionary. Then make your own sentences below.

1. _____.

2. _____.

3. _____.

227. SEMICIRCLE

Meaning:
It is half of a circle or an arrangement of people or things that forms half of a circle.

Examples:
1. The children sat in a *semicircle*.
2. The houses are built in a *semicircle*.

To understand more look it up in a dictionary. Then make your own sentences below.

1. _____.

2. _____.

3. _____.

228. LOUNGE

Meaning:
A lounge is a comfortable room for relaxing in a public building such as a hotel or airport.

Examples:
1. There were not enough seats in the *lounge* for all the guests.
2. The hotel has a television *lounge*.

To understand more look it up in a dictionary. Then make your own sentences below.

1. _____.
2. _____.
3. _____.

229. FUMBLE

Meaning:
This word means to search for something by reaching or touching with your fingers in an awkward or clumsy way.

Examples:
1. He *fumbled* around for the light switch when she woke up in the middle of the night.
2. She *fumbled* with her keys as she tried to unlock the door.

To understand more look it up in a dictionary. Then make your own sentences below.

1. _____.
2. _____.
3. _____.

230. RESIDENT

Meaning:
A resident is someone who lives in a particular place usually for a long period of time.

here are two examples of potential use,
1. Several tribes are *resident* in this part of the country.
2. She is a *resident* of New York.

To understand more look it up in a dictionary. Then make your own sentences below.

1. _____.
2. _____.
3. _____.

231. ENSURE

Meaning:
To ensure is to make something sure or certain to happen.

Examples:
1. They took steps to *ensure* the safety of the passengers.
2. We want to *ensure* that it doesn't happen again.

To understand more look it up in a dictionary. Then make your own sentences below.

1. _____.
2. _____.
3. _____.

232. PREVENT

Meaning:
This means to stop something from happening or to stop someone from doing something.

Examples :
1. Seatbelts in cars often *prevent* serious injuries.
2. He grabbed my arm to *prevent* me from falling.

To understand more look it up in a dictionary. Then make your own sentences below.

1. _____.
2. _____.
3. _____.

233. TO BAN

Meaning:
To refuse to allow someone to do something, go somewhere, or be a participant.

Examples:
1. The city has *banned* smoking in all public buildings.
2. He was *banned* from entering the building.

To understand more look it up in a dictionary. Then make your own sentences below.

1. _____.
2. _____.
3. _____.

234. GUILTY

Meaning:
To be guilty is to feel or be responsible for committing a crime or doing something bad or wrong.

Examples:
1. Do you think he's innocent or *guilty*?
2. The children exchanged *guilty* looks.

To understand more look it up in a dictionary. Then make your own sentences below.

1. _____.

2. _____.

3. _____.

235. INSTANT

Meaning:
An instant is a very short period of time.

Examples:
1. He became an *instant* celebrity with the publication of his first novel.
2. The Internet provides *instant* access to an enormous amount of information.

To understand more look it up in a dictionary. Then make your own sentences below.

1. _____.

2. _____.

3. _____.

236. AGONY

Meaning:
It is an extreme physical or mental pain or suffering, or a period of such suffering.

Examples:
1. She was in terrible *agony* after breaking her leg.
2. The medicine relieves the *agony* of muscle cramps very quickly.

To understand more look it up in a dictionary. Then make your own sentences below.

1. _____.

2. _____.

3. _____.

237. TO OBJECT

Meaning:
To object something is to disagree with something or oppose something

Examples:
1. No one *objected* when the paintings were removed.
2. He *objected* that the chair was too big to fit in the car.

To understand more look it up in a dictionary. Then make your own sentences below.

1. _____.

2. _____.

3. _____.

238. WEIRD

Meaning:
Something is weird when it is strange and different from anything natural or ordinary.

Examples:
1. She listens to some really **weird** music.
2. My little brother acts **weird** sometimes.

To understand more look it up in a dictionary. Then make your own sentences below.

1. _____.
2. _____.
3. _____.

239. TO ADAPT

Meaning:
To adapt is to change or change something to meet different situations.

Examples :
1. When children go to a different school, it usually takes them a while to *adapt.*
2. The camera has been *adapted* for underwater use.

To understand more look it up in a dictionary. Then make your own sentences below.

1. _____.
2. _____.
3. _____.

240. MASSIVE

Meaning:
Something is massive when it is very large in size, amount, or degree.

Examples:
1. A *massive* effort will be required to clean up the debris.
2. He suffered a *massive* heart attack.

To understand more look it up in a dictionary. Then make your own sentences below.

1. _____.

2. _____.

3. _____.

TREASURE BOX 16: THINK IN ENGLISH.

This takes some getting used to, but soon you will find it becoming a second nature.
The right words or phrases will come faster and easier then.

EXERCISE 32

Use the correct form of these words to fill in the gaps;

DIMENSION, CONTRAST, INFECT, LEGIBLE, SUSPECT, TRAUMA

1. The _____ vehicle was reported to the police.

2. They were unable to prevent bacteria from _____ the wound.

3. His essay _____ his life in America with/to life in India.

4. She never fully recovered from the _____ she suffered during her childhood.

5. He doesn't write _____ at all and it is very difficult to read his writings.

6. The social/political/religious _____ of the problem must also be taken into account.

EXERCISE 33

A Hotel Experience

I was Staying at a hotel in Kawaguchi, Japan. I couldn't sleep because the television in the residents' lounge was so loud. As I could see from the top of the stairs, the lounge was in total darkness, so I crept downstairs in my pajamas. I went to the TV and after some fumbling with the knobs I managed to switch it off.

As I turned to leave, I suddenly became aware of a semi-circle of people sitting in the dark who, up until that moment, had been enjoying a television program.

Mark the best choice from **a** to **d**.

1. 'Lounge' is ....
    a. kind of taxi in the airport etc.
    b. small room for workers
    c. public sitting room in a hotel
    d. special case for television

2. To 'creep' means to ....
    a. run quickly
    b. jump off
    c. shout out
    d. move quietly

3. To '............' means to move the hands awkwardly to do something or to find something.
    a. fumble
    b. manage
    c. switch
    d. reside

4. A 'knob' is a .....
   a. hotel room
   b. small TV
   c. round handle
   d. special table

5. Aware here means ....
   a. to manage
   b. having knowledge or conscious
   c. to switch
   d. to jump into something

6. Resident means..............
   a. One who lives or resides in a particular place permanently or for an extended period.
   b. a public living room
   c. anyone who uses management skills or holds the organizational title
   d. continuing or enduring without fundamental or marked change

7. Semi circle means.............................
   a. a prolonged exposure to the sun
   b. record of some proceedings
   c. a half of a circle
   d. The way houses are built.

EXERCISE 34

Match the following words with the correct definitions.

ENSURE, PREVENT, GUILTY, AGONY, INSTANT, BAN

1. A very short period of time.

2. To forbid (someone) from doing or being part of something.

3. Extreme mental or physical pain.

4. Responsible for committing a crime or doing something bad or wrong.

5. To stop someone or something from doing something.

6. To make (something) sure, certain, or safe.

241. ENFORCE

Meaning:
To enforce is to make people obey a law, or to make a particular situation happen or be accepted.

here are two examples of potential use;
1. Police will be *enforcing* the parking ban.
2. This is not an *enforceable* contract.

To understand more look it up in a dictionary. Then make your own sentences below.

1. _____.
2. _____.
3. _____.

242. SIGNIFICANT

Meaning:
Something is significant when it is large enough to be noticed or very important.

Examples :
1. A *significant* number of customers complained about the service.
2. He won a *significant* amount of money.

To understand more look it up in a dictionary. Then make your own sentences below.

1. _____.
2. _____.
3. _____.

243. RESEARCH

Meaning:
This is a detailed study of a subject in order to discover information or achieve a new understanding of it

Examples:
1. Recent *research* shows that the disease is caused in part by bad nutrition.
2. He did a lot of *research* before buying his car.

To understand more look it up in a dictionary. Then make your own sentences below.

1. _____.
2. _____.
3. _____.

244. TOPIC

Meaning:
A topic is someone or something that people talk or write about.

Examples
1. He is comfortable discussing a wide range of *topics*.
2. The new boss has been the main *topic of* conversation.

To understand more look it up in a dictionary. Then make your own sentences below.

1. _____.
2. _____.
3. _____.

245. TO AID

Meaning:
Aid is often used to refer to help given in the form of food, money, medical supplies, etc., to a country or group of people that is in need or because of an emergency.

Examples:
1. He jumped into the water to **aid** the drowning child.
2. His research **aided** *in* the discovery of a new treatment for cancer.

To understand more look it up in a dictionary. Then make your own sentences below.

1. _____.
2. _____.
3. _____.

246. DELEGATE

Meaning:
A delegate is a person chosen or elected by a group to represent the group. It also means to give a job or responsibility to someone instead of doing it yourself.

Examples:
1. A manager should **delegate** authority to the best employees.
2. He was **delegated** by the town to take care of the monument.

To understand more look it up in a dictionary. Then make your own sentences below.

1. _____.
2. _____.
3. _____.

247. MANDATORY

Meaning:
Something that is mandatory must be done, or is demanded by law.

Examples:
1. This meeting is **mandatory** for all employees. [=all employees must go to this meeting].
2. The **mandatory** fine for littering is $200. [=everyone caught littering must pay $200].

To understand more look it up in a dictionary. Then make your own sentences below.

1. _____.

2. _____.

3. _____.

248. ADDICTION

Meaning:
Addiction is the need or strong desire to do or to have something harmful.

Examples:
1. He has an **addiction** *to* playing the lottery.
2. He devotes his summers to his surfing **addiction**.

To understand more look it up in a dictionary. Then make your own sentences below.

1. _____.

2. _____.

3. _____.

249. TREATMENT

Meaning:
This is the act, manner, or method of handling or dealing with someone or something.
It is also the use of drugs, exercises, etc. to cure a person of an illness or injury.

Examples :
1. We want to ensure equal *treatment* for everyone.
2. Previous *treatments* of this topic have ignored some key issues.
3. The patient required immediate medical *treatment*.

To understand more look it up in a dictionary. Then make your own sentences below.

1. _____.

2. _____.

3. _____.

250. UNDERGROUND

Meaning:
Underground is something situated or located below the surface of the earth.
It also means something that secret or hidden, usually because it is illegal.

Examples:
1. I've ridden on the New York subway, the Paris Metro, and the London *Underground*.
2. The drugs are supplied through an *underground* network.
3. They had been living *underground* as fugitives.

To understand more look it up in a dictionary. Then make your own sentences below.

1. _____.

2. _____.

3. _____.

251. TO VANISH

Meaning:
It means to suddenly disappear entirely without a clear explanation or to stop existing

Examples:
1. The missing girl *vanished* without a trace a year ago.
2. The custom has all *vanished*.

To understand more look it up in a dictionary. Then make your own sentences below.

1. _____.

2. _____.

3. _____.

252. NOMINEE

Meaning:
A nominee is a person who has been officially chosen for a position, an honor, or election.

Examples:
1. She is one of the *nominees* for Best Actress.
2. He is the President's *nominee* for Attorney General.

To understand more look it up in a dictionary. Then make your own sentences below.

1. _____.

2. _____.

3. _____.

253. TO REVIVE

Meaning:
To revive is to bring something back to life, health or existence.

Examples:
1. The doctors were trying to *revive* the patient.
2. The family is trying to *revive* an old custom.

To understand more look it up in a dictionary. Then make your own sentences below.

1. _____.

2. _____.

3. _____.

254. PROPOSAL

Meaning:
A proposal is something such as a plan or suggestion that is presented to a person or group of people to consider.

Examples :
1. The committee is reviewing the *proposal* for the new restaurant.
2. They rejected/accepted/considered/approved my business *proposal.*

To understand more look it up in a dictionary. Then make your own sentences below.

1. _____.

2. _____.

3. _____.

255. FLEXIBLE

Meaning:
To be flexible is to be able to bend or be bent easily without breaking or be able to change or be changed easily according to the situation.

Examples:
1. She's been doing exercises to become stronger and more *flexible*.
2. Whatever you want to do is fine with me, I'm *flexible*.

To understand more look it up in a dictionary. Then make your own sentences below.

1. _____.

2. _____.

3. _____.

TREASURE BOX 17: WATCH AND IMITATE.

Observe the mouth movements of those who speak English well and try to imitate them. When you are watching television, observe the mouth movements of the speakers. Repeat what they are saying, while imitating the intonation and rhythm of their speech.

256. IMPAIR

Meaning:
To impair is to damage or weaken something so that it is less effective:

Examples:
1. Smoking can *impair* your health.
2. The disease causes *impaired* vision/hearing in elderly people.

To understand more look it up in a dictionary. Then make your own sentences below.

1. _____.
2. _____.
3. _____.

257. CHAOS

Meaning:
Chaos is a state of complete confusion and disorder in which behavior and events are not controlled by anything.

Examples:
1. The loss of electricity caused *chaos* throughout the city.
2. When the police arrived, the street was in total/complete/absolute *chaos.*

To understand more look it up in a dictionary. Then make your own sentences below.

1. _____.
2. _____.
3. _____.

258. FUNCTION

Meaning:
Function of a thing is the special purpose or activity for which a thing exists or is used.

Examples:
1. He believes that the true *function* of art is to tell the truth.
2. His job combines the *functions* of a manager and a worker.

To understand more look it up in a dictionary. Then make your own sentences below.

1. _____.

2. _____.

3. _____.

259. RENOWN

Meaning:
This word means the quality of being widely known or acclaimed or famous.

Example
1. That Italian restaurant is *renowned* for its wine list.
2. He is a *renowned* scientist.

To understand more look it up in a dictionary. Then make your own sentences below.

1. _____.

2. _____.

3. _____.

260. SUBSEQUENT

Meaning:
Something is subsequent to another when it happens after something else.

Examples.
1. Her work had a great influence on **subsequent** generations.
2. She graduated from college and **subsequently** moved to New York.

Check it out in your dictionary for more examples and understanding.

To understand more look it up in a dictionary. Then make your own sentences below.

1. _____.

2. _____.

3. _____.

EXERCISE 35

Match the following words with the appropriate definition.

ADAPT, MASSIVE, ENFORCE, SIGNIFICANT, WEIRD, OBJECT

1. To impose (a course of action) upon a person or a group of people is...........

2. To make suitable to requirements or conditions, adjust or modify fittingly is............

3. To express or feel disapproval, dislike, or distaste is.....................

4. Large in scale, amount, or degree is.................

5. Important or having or likely to have influence or effect is.................

6. of strange, odd or extraordinary character is....................

EXERCISE 36

Match the following words with the appropriate definition.

RESEARCH, TOPIC, AID, MANDATORY, ADDICTION, DELEGATE

1. Required or commanded by authority; obligatory ---------------------

2. To assign or entrust responsibility or authority to another --------------

3. The collecting of information about a particular subject ---------------

4. Someone or something that people talk or write about ------------------

5. To provide what is useful or necessary ---------------------------------

6. A strong and harmful need to regularly have something or do something -------

EXERCISE 37

Match the following words with the appropriate definitions.

TREATMENT, UNDERGROUND, VANISH, NOMINEE, REVIVE, PROPOSAL

1. To disappear, especially suddenly or mysteriously.

2. To bring back or to return to life or consciousness.

3. The act, manner, or method of handling or dealing with someone or something.

4. A person or organization named to act on behalf of someone else.

5. Something offered as new offerings for investors included several index funds.

6. Hidden or concealed or relating to an organization involved in secret or illegal activity.

EXERCISE 38

The words in bold are in the wrong places, put them in the appropriate places.

1. The action for which a person or thing is particularly fitted or employed. **CHAOS**

2. Following in time or order; succeeding. **IMPAIR**

3. Capable of being bent repeatedly without injury or damage. **FUNCTION**

4. To cause to diminish, as in strength, value, or quality. **SUBSEQUENT**

5. The quality of being widely honored and acclaimed; fame. **FLEXIBLE**

6. A condition or place of great disorder or confusion. **RENOWN**

261. TO OBTAIN

Meaning:
This word means to get or gain possession of something by a planned effort.

Examples:
1. The information may be difficult to *obtain*.
2. They've *obtained* the necessary permission to enter into the house.

To understand more look it up in a dictionary. Then make your own sentences below.

1. _____.

2. _____.

3. _____.

262. ABSTAIN

Meaning:
To abstain from doing something is to choose not to do it.

Examples:
1. I need to *abstain* from eating for at least 12 hours before my blood test.
2. People are *abstaining* from drinking when they drive.

To understand more look it up in a dictionary. Then make your own sentences below.

1. _____.

2. _____.

3. _____.

263. GENERATE

Meaning:
To generate something is to produce (something) or cause (something) to be produced.

Examples:
1. This business should *generate* a lot of revenue.
2. They have been unable to *generate* much support for their proposals.

To understand more look it up in a dictionary. Then make your own sentences below.

1. _____.
2. _____.
3. _____.

264. PROFESSIONAL

Meaning:
A professional is a person who has a job that needs skill, education, or training.

Examples:
1. Do you have any *professional* experience?
2. Her presentation was very *professional*.

To understand more look it up in a dictionary. Then make your own sentences below.

1. _____.
2. _____.
3. _____.

265. STUMBLE

Meaning:
To stumble is to hit your foot on something when you are walking or running so that you fall or almost fall. It also means to begin to have problems after a time of success.

Examples:
1. She usually *stumbles* out of bed around 7:00 am.
2. The economy has *stumbled* in recent months.

To understand more look it up in a dictionary. Then make your own sentences below.

1. _____.

2. _____.

3. _____.

266. NEGLIGENCE

Meaning:
Negligence is failing to be careful enough or to give enough attention to your responsibilities, especially when it results in harm or loss to others

Examples:
1. The company was charged with *negligence* in the manufacturing of the defective tires.
2. Medical *negligence* may be the cause of Michael Jackson's death.

To understand more look it up in a dictionary. Then make your own sentences below.

1. _____.

2. _____.

3. _____.

267. UNLIKELY

Meaning:
Something is unlikely when it is not expected to happen or not true.

Examples:
1. It is *unlikely* that the company will survive more than another year.
2. A big city is an *unlikely* place to find wildlife.

To understand more look it up in a dictionary. Then make your own sentences below.

1. _____.

2. _____.

3. _____.

268. DILUTE

Meaning:
To dilute a liquid means to make it weaker by mixing it with water or another liquid.

Examples:
1. You can *dilute* the medicine with water.
2. The hiring of the new CEO *diluted* the power of the company's president.

To understand more look it up in a dictionary. Then make your own sentences below.

1. _____.

2. _____.

3. _____.

269. TO BOND

Meaning:
To bond means to stick materials together, usually using glue or to develop a close and lasting relationship.

Examples:
1. We were strangers at first, but we **bonded** *with* each other quickly.
2. The pieces of wood **bonded** to each other well.

To understand more look it up in a dictionary. Then make your own sentences below.

1. _____.

2. _____.

3. _____.

270. TO GAMBLE

Meaning:
To gamble is to do something that you think is worth doing although it might not succeed or you might lose money.

Examples:
1. She thought starting her own business was a **gamble** so she gave up the idea.
2. Many people are willing to take a **gamble** on the new medical treatment.

To understand more look it up in a dictionary. Then make your own sentences below.

1. _____.

2. _____.

3. _____.

TREASURE BOX 18: LISTEN TO THE 'MUSIC' OF ENGLISH.

Do not use the 'music' of your native language when you speak English. Each language has its own way of 'singing'. Listen to the 'music' of English and understand the rhythm. It will help you connect during your conversations

271. RADIANT

Meaning:
Radiant means bright and shining or having an attractive quality of happiness.

Example:
a. She always has a *radiant* smile.
b. She looked *radiant* at her wedding.
c. They were fascinated by the *radiant* blue skies.

Look this word up in a dictionary for more possible use.

To understand more look it up in a dictionary. Then make your own sentences below.

1. _____.

2. _____.

3. _____.

272. TO MANIPULATE

Meaning:
This word means to influence or control someone to your advantage, often without that person knowing it.

Examples:
1. The program was designed to organize and **manipulate** large amount of data.
2. She knows how to *manipulate* her parents to get what she wants.

To understand more look it up in a dictionary. Then make your own sentences below.

1. _____.
2. _____.
3. _____.

273. TO INTIMIDATE

Meaning:
To intimidate someone is to frighten or threaten the person.

Examples:
1. He is one of the most *intimidating* men I have ever met.
2. I feel less *intimidated* now than I did when I started the job.

To understand more look it up in a dictionary. Then make your own sentences below.

1. _____.
2. _____.
3. _____.

274. SYNONYM

Meaning:
A synonym is a word or phrase that has the same or nearly the same meaning as another word or phrase in the same language.

Examples:
1. "Small" is a **synonym** of "little.
2. Can you think of a *synonym* for original?
3. He is a tyrant whose name has become a *synonym* for oppression.

To understand more look it up in a dictionary. Then make your own sentences below.

1. _____.

2. _____.

3. _____.

275. ANTONYM

Meaning:
An antonym is a word or phrase whose meaning is the opposite of another word or phrase in the same language.

Examples:
1. Hot" and "cold" are *antonyms*.
2. Fast is an *antonym* of slow.

To understand more look it up in a dictionary. Then make your own sentences below.

1. _____.

2. _____.

3. _____.

276. TO COMPENSATE

Meaning:
To compensate means to pay someone money in exchange for work done, for something lost or damaged, or for some inconvenience.

Examples:
1. She was *compensated* for the loss of her arm in the accident.
2. Management *compensated* us for the extra time we worked.

To understand more look it up in a dictionary. Then make your own sentences below.

1. _____.

2. _____.

3. _____.

277. SPECIFIC

Meaning:
To be specific means clearly and exactly presented or stated.

Examples:
1. Is there anything **specific** you want for dinner?
2. We were each given a *specific* topic to talk about.

To understand more look it up in a dictionary. Then make your own sentences below.

1. _____.

2. _____.

3. _____.

278. To Discover

Meaning:
To discover means to find something for the first time, or something that had not been known before.

Examples:
1. It took her several weeks to **discover** the solution.
2. During her career she was responsible for **discovering** many famous musicians.

To understand more look it up in a dictionary. Then make your own sentences below.

1. _____.

2. _____.

3. _____.

279. To Perceive

Meaning:
To perceive something means to notice, think of or become aware of it by using sight, sound, touch, taste, or smell.

Examples:
1. The detective **perceived** a change in the suspect's attitude.
2. He is **perceived** as one of the best players in baseball.

To understand more look it up in a dictionary. Then make your own sentences below.

1. _____.

2. _____.

3. _____.

280. To Manifest

Meaning:
To manifest means to clearly reveal its presence or make an appearance.

Examples :
1. Both sides have **manifested** a stubborn unwillingness to compromise.
2. Love *manifests* itself in many different ways.

To understand more look it up in a dictionary. Then make your own sentences below.

1. _____.

2. _____.

3. _____.

EXERCISE 39

Fill in the gaps with the appropriate form of the following words.

OBTAIN ABSTAIN GENERATE PROFESSION STUMBLE NEGLIGENCE

1. Higher education always seems to .... controversy.

2. The horse .... and almost fell.

3. These ideas no longer .... for our generation.

4. The downfall of the company was brought about by many .... of the staff.

5. He decided to .... from taking part in the discussion.

6. I was impressed by the calm and .... way she handled the crisis.

EXERCISE 40

Write one word with the same meaning to each of the following words.

1. UNLIKELY   ----------------------------

2. TO DILUTE   ----------------------------

3. TO BOND   ----------------------------

4. TO GAMBLE   ----------------------------

5. ASSET   ----------------------------

6. RADIANT   ----------------------------

EXERCISE 41

Give the synonyms and antonyms of the following words

WORDS	**SYNONYMS**	**ANTONYMS**
1. MANIPULATE	....	....
2. INTIMIDATE	....	....
3. SYNONYM	....	....
4. ANTONYM	....	....
5. COMPENSATE	....	....
6. SPECIFIC	....	....

281. TO EXIST

Meaning:
If something exists, it is actually present under certain circumstances or in a specified place.

Examples:
1. She believes that ghosts really do *exist.*
2. Does life *exist* on Mars?

To understand more look it up in a dictionary. Then make your own sentences below.

1. _____.
2. _____.
3. _____.

282. EFFECTIVE

Meaning:
If someone or something is effective, they do something well and produce the results that were intended.

Examples:
1. It's a simple but *effective* technique.
2. He gave an *effective* speech.

To understand more look it up in a dictionary. Then make your own sentences below.

1. _____.
2. _____.
3. _____.

283. CIRCUMSTANCE

Meaning:
The circumstances of an event are the way it happened or the causes of it.

Examples :
1. The *circumstances* of his death are suspicious.
2. Due to *circumstances* beyond our control, the flight is canceled.

To understand more look it up in a dictionary. Then make your own sentences below.

1. _____.
2. _____.
3. _____.

284. TRADITIONAL

Meaning:
Traditional means following or belonging to the ways of behaving or beliefs that have been established for a long time by the people in a particular group or culture.

Examples:
1. It is *traditional* to eat turkey and cranberry sauce on Thanksgiving.
2. She loves wearing *traditional* Japanese kimono for special occasion.

To understand more look it up in a dictionary. Then make your own sentences below.

1. _____.
2. _____.
3. _____.

285. PARTICIPATE

Meaning:
To participate means to take part in an activity or event with others.

Examples:
1. Most people joined the game, but a few chose not to *participate*.
2. He is known for his active *participation* in community affairs.

To understand more look it up in a dictionary. Then make your own sentences below.

1. _____.

2. _____.

3. _____.

TREASURE BOX 19: DON'T GIVE UP!

Some students say "I've been studying for 3, 4, 5 years, but still I can't speak well". My advice is, continue learning and you may try various ways of doing it to avoid boredom. You can always start all over again and again, even going back to the basics.

286. HENCEFORTH

Meaning:
Henceforth means starting from this time.

Examples:
1. *Henceforth*, supervisors will report directly to the manager.
2. She announced that *henceforth* she would be running the company.

To understand more look it up in a dictionary. Then make your own sentences below.

1. _____.
2. _____.
3. _____.

287. ENCOUNTER

Meaning:
An encounter is meeting someone unexpectedly or experiencing something unpleasant.

Examples:
1. We *encountered* problems early in the project.
2. The pilot told us that we might *encounter* turbulence during the flight.

To understand more look it up in a dictionary. Then make your own sentences below.

1. _____.
2. _____.
3. _____.

288. IGNITE

Meaning:
Ignite means to start burning, or to cause something to start burning. It also means to give life or energy to someone or something.

Examples :
1. The fire was *ignited* by sparks.
2. Three wins in a row *ignited* the team.

To understand more look it up in a dictionary. Then make your own sentences below.

1. _____.

2. _____.

3. _____.

289. TIMID

Meaning:
It means to be easily frightened, not brave or Lacking self-confidence.

Examples:
1. she's very *timid* and shy when meeting strangers.
2. He gave her a *timid* smile.

To understand more look it up in a dictionary. Then make your own sentences below.

1. _____.

2. _____.

3. _____.

290. MOMENTUM

Meaning:
The strength or force that something has when it is moving.

Examples:
1. The truck gained *momentum* as it rolled down the hill.
2. The truck lost *momentum* as it rolled up the hill.
3. The company has had a successful year and hopes to maintain its *momentum* by introducing new products.

To understand more look it up in a dictionary. Then make your own sentences below.

1. _____.

2. _____.

3. _____.

291. NARRATIVE

Meaning:
Narrative is a particular way of explaining or understanding events.

Examples:
1. He is writing a detailed *narrative* of his life on the island.
2. People have questioned the accuracy of his *narrative*.

To understand more look it up in a dictionary. Then make your own sentences below.

1. _____.

2. _____.

3. _____.

292. BEGINNING

Meaning:
The point or time at which something begins, a starting point or the first part of something

Examples:
1. He has been working there since the **beginning** of the year.
2. Go back to the **beginning** of the song.
3. The school has courses for **beginning**, intermediate, and advanced students.

To understand more look it up in a dictionary. Then make your own sentences below.

1. _____.

2. _____.

3. _____.

293. RESOLUTION

Meanings:
1. The ability of a device to show an image clearly and with a lot of detail.
2. A promise to yourself that you will make a serious effort to do something that you should do.

Examples:
a. He made a **resolution** **t**o lose weight.
b. Her New Year's **resolution** is to exercise regularly.
c. A high-**resolution** copier/monitor/camera/computer.

To understand more look it up in a dictionary. Then make your own sentences below.

1. _____.

2. _____.

3. _____.

294. INFLUENCE

Meanings:
It means the power to cause someone to change a behavior, belief, or opinion, or to cause something to be changed

Examples:
Dr. Martin Luther King's speech *influenced* the course of American history.

To understand more look it up in a dictionary. Then make your own sentences below.

1. _____.

2. _____.

3. _____.

295. ATTITUDE

Meaning:
The way you feel about something or someone, or a particular feeling or opinion

Example:
Start each day with a positive *attitude*.

To understand more look it up in a dictionary. Then make your own sentences below.

1. _____.

2. _____.

3. _____.

296. PRESUMPTUOUS

Meaning:

A person who is presumptuous shows little respect for others by doing things they have no right to do and is excessively confident.

Examples:

a. They couldn't believe how *presumptuous* their neighbor was in assuming that she was invited to their party.

b. Ever since he was a little child, he had been known to be *presumptuous*, forcing his way into any situation which caught his eye.

c. The *presumptuous* doctor didn't even bother to explain to me the treatment that I would be receiving.

To understand more look it up in a dictionary. Then make your own sentences below.

1. _____.

2. _____.

3. _____.

297. OCCUPY

Meaning:
To occupy is to move into and take control or possession, fill or be in a place or space or to use an amount of time.

Examples:
1. They have *occupied* the apartment for three years.
2. That family trip *occupies* a special place in my memory.
3. Studying *occupies* nearly all of my time on the weekends.

To understand more look it up in a dictionary. Then make your own sentences below.

1. _____.

2. _____.

3. _____.

298. SOLITARY

Meanings:
1. It means, living, or going alone or without companions.
2. One who lives or seeks to live a lonely life.

Examples:
a. He took a *solitary* walk on the beach.
b. He's a very *solitary* man.
c. The prisoner was kept in *solitary*.

To understand more look it up in a dictionary. Then make your own sentences below.

1. _____.

2. _____.

3. _____.

299. EMPHASIZE

Meaning:
To give special attention to something.

Examples:
a. Their father always *emphasized* the importance of discipline.
b. He tried to *emphasize* that he hadn't meant to offend anyone.

To understand more look it up in a dictionary. Then make your own sentences below.

1. _____.

2. _____.

3. _____.

300. IMMEDIATE

Meanings:
1. Happening or done without delay.
2. Having no other person or thing in between.

Examples:
1. The new restaurant was an *immediate* success.
2. They have evacuated everyone in the *immediate* area of the wildfire.
3. Hospital visits are limited to *immediate* family.

To understand more look it up in a dictionary. Then make your own sentences below.

1. _____.

2. _____.

3. _____.

TREASURE BOX 20 : SET GOALS

> Set goals, something that you are trying to do or achieve with English.
> This will surely motivate you.

EXERCISE 42

Match the words with the appropriate definitions

NARRATIVE, DISCOVER, PERCEIVE, MANIFEST, EXIST, EFFECTIVE, CIRCUMSTANCE,

1. To notice, think or become aware of something or someone is ....

2. The way something happens : the specific details of an event is ....

3. To see, find, or become aware of something for the first time is ....

4. To continue to be or to live or to be real...

5. Easy to understand or recognize or visible...

6. Producing a result that is wanted or having an intended effect ....

7. A particular way of explaining or understanding events ....

EXERCISE 43

Give the Synonyms and antonyms of these words.

	SYNONYM	**ANTONYM**
1. RESOLUTION	....	....
2. BEGINNING	....	....
3. INFLUENCE	....	....
4. HAMMER	....	....
5. ATTITUDE	....	....
6. MOMENTUM	....	....
7. TMID	....	....
8. IGNITE	....	....
9. ENCOUNTER	....	....
10. HENCEFORTH	....	....
11. PARTICIPATE	....	....
12. TRADITIONAL	....	....

301. POSTPONE

Meaning:
It means to delay an event or arrange for it to take place at a later time.

Examples:
The baseball game was *postponed* until/to tomorrow because of rain.

To understand more look it up in a dictionary. Then make your own sentences below.

1. _____.

2. _____.

3. _____.

302. EXTEND

Meanings:
1. To become longer or to be able to become longer or to make something longer or greater.
2. To offer feelings, such as an apology to someone.

Examples:
a. The table measures eight meter long when it is fully *extended*.
b. She *extended* her visit by a couple of weeks.
c. They *extended* a warm welcome to us.

To understand more look it up in a dictionary. Then make your own sentences below.

1. _____.

2. _____.

3. _____.

303. REGULATE

Meanings:
1. To set or adjust or control the amount, degree, or rate of something.
2. To bring something under the control of authority or government.

Examples:
a. The thermostat *regulates* the room's temperature.
b. We need better laws to *regulate* the content of the Internet.
c. The government *regulates* foreign trade.

To understand more look it up in a dictionary. Then make your own sentences below.

1. _____.
2. _____.
3. _____.

304. SHATTER

Meaning:
To break or be broken into many small pieces.

Examples:
1. The windshield *shattered* when the bullet went through the glass.
2. Reading about all the necessary paperwork and licenses needed before opening a business, *shattered* his entrepreneurial dreams.

To understand more look it up in a dictionary. Then make your own sentences below.

1. _____.
2. _____.
3. _____.

305. LAMENT

Meaning:
To express grief or deep regret about something or action.

Examples:
a. They *lamented* the fact that they didn't study harder in school.
b. She may unfortunately have to *lament* her carelessness for a long time.

To understand more look it up in a dictionary. Then make your own sentences below.

1. _____.

2. _____.

3. _____.

306. FLAMBOYANT

Meaning:
Having a very noticeable quality that attracts a lot of attention.

Examples:
a. A *flamboyant* performer was at the station.
b. The *flamboyant* gestures of the conductor attracts people's attention.
c. A lot of models wearing *flamboyant* clothes were at the show.

To understand more look it up in a dictionary. Then make your own sentences below.

1. _____.

2. _____.

3. _____.

307. COMMUNITY

Meanings:
1. A group of people who live in the same area such as a city, town, or neighborhood.
2. A group of people who have the same interests, religion, race, etc.
3. A group of nations — usually singular.

Examples:
a. The festival was a great way for the local *community* to get together.
b. An artistic/business/medical *community*.
c. The international *community*.

To understand more look it up in a dictionary. Then make your own sentences below.

1. _____.
2. _____.
3. _____.

308. REMAIN

Meaning:
It means to stay in the same place or with the same person or group or to stay behind or unchanged.

Examples:
a. Only a little *remained* after the fire.
b. I *remained* behind after the class had ended.
c. Organic *remains* are good source of energy.

To understand more look it up in a dictionary. Then make your own sentences below.

1. _____.
2. _____.
3. _____.

309. TOGETHER

Meanings and Examples :
1. To be with each other.
   The old friends were *together* again after many long years apart.
2. In or into one group, mixture, piece, etc.
   They gathered *together* to celebrate.
3. When people are in a close relationship.
   They've been *together* for almost five years.
4. When two or more people or things touch.
   The doors banged *together*.
5. When things happen at the same time.
   They all cheered *together*.

To understand more look it up in a dictionary. Then make your own sentences below.

1. _____.
2. _____.
3. _____.

310. BEAUTY

Meanings and Examples:
1. The quality of being physically attractive.
   Her *beauty* is beyond compare.
2. A good or appealing part of something.
   The *beauty* of the game is that everyone can play.

To understand more look it up in a dictionary. Then make your own sentences below.

1. _____.
2. _____.
3. _____.

311. APTITUDE

Meaning:
An aptitude is natural ability or skill.

Example:
My son has no *aptitude* for sports.

To understand more look it up in a dictionary. Then make your own sentences below.

1. _____.

2. _____.

3. _____.

312. IRRESISTIBLE

Meaning:
It means impossible to refuse, oppose, or avoid because too pleasant, attractive, or strong.

Examples:
a. I wasn't going to have dessert, but the pie proved *irresistible*.
b. she looked *irresistible* in her new dress

To understand more look it up in a dictionary. Then make your own sentences below.

1. _____.

2. _____.

3. _____.

313. BROAD

Meanings and Examples:
1. Large or wide from one side to the other.
   He has **broad** shoulders.
2. Including or involving many things or people.
   The store has a **broad** selection of coats
3. Concerning the main parts of something.
   The **broad** outlines of a problem.

To understand more look it up in a dictionary. Then make your own sentences below.

1. _____.
2. _____.
3. _____.

314. PURCHASE

Meaning and Examples:
it means to get obtain something by paying money for it.
It is a formal word for the word **"buy"**.

a. He **purchased** a new suit for one hundred dollars.
b. Souvenirs can be **purchased** at the gift shop.

To understand more look it up in a dictionary. Then make your own sentences below.

1. _____.
2. _____.
3. _____.

315. PRIVILEDGE

Meanings and Examples:
1. A right or benefit that is given to some people and not to others.
   Good health care should be a right and not a *privilege*.
2. A special opportunity to do something that makes one proud.
   Meeting the President was a *privilege*.

To understand more look it up in a dictionary. Then make your own sentences below.

1. _____.

2. _____.

3. _____.

TREASURE BOX 21: TREAT YOURSELF

Treat yourself for a job well done after you studied well and continue to do it. This will also motivate you.

316. REQUIREMENT

Meaning and Example:
Requirement is something that is needed or that must be done.
He has met the basic or minimum *requirements* for graduation.

To understand more look it up in a dictionary. Then make your own sentences below.

1. _____.

2. _____.

3. _____.

317. SADDLE

Meanings and Examples:
As a noun, it means a leather-covered seat that is put on the back of a horse or a seat on a bicycle or motorcycle.
As a verb, it means to put a saddle on a horse.

a. He *saddled* his horse and mounted it.
b. My bike needs a new *saddle*.

To understand more look it up in a dictionary. Then make your own sentences below.

1. _____.
2. _____.
3. _____.

318. AGILE

Meanings and Examples:
Agile means to be able to move quickly and easily, quick, smart, and clever.

a.   She is the most *agile* athlete on the team.
b.   Leopards are very fast and *agile*.

To understand more look it up in a dictionary. Then make your own sentences below.

1. _____.
2. _____.
3. _____.

319. AFFIRM

Meanings and Examples:
1. To affirm means, to say that something is true in a confident way
    We cannot *affirm* that this painting is genuine.
2. It can also mean to decide that the judgment of another court is correct.
    The decision was *affirmed* by a higher court.

To understand more look it up in a dictionary. Then make your own sentences below.

1. _____.

2. _____.

3. _____.

320. COMPATIBLE

Meaning and Examples:
It is the ability to exist together without trouble or conflict or going together well.

a. My roommate and I are very *compatible*.
b. This printer is *compatible* with most PCs.

To understand more look it up in a dictionary. Then make your own sentences below.

1. _____.

2. _____.

3. _____.

EXERCISE 44

Fill the following gaps with the appropriate form of the following words.

PRESUMPTUOUS, SOLITARY, OCCUPY, EMPHASIZE, IMMEDIATE, POSTPONE, EXTEND, REGULATE, SHATTER, LAMENT, COMMUNITY, FLAMBOYANT

1. She .... herself with her butterfly collection.

2. Dr. Jones .... exercise in addition to a change in diet.

3. Paul was a shy, pleasant ....man, his evenings were spent in .... drinking.

4. Relief agencies say the .... problem is not a lack of food, but transportation.

5. The trip has been .... twice.

6. The governor found it ....that the mayor called him by his first name.

7. Live animal research is more tightly .... in Britain than anywhere else in the world.

8. Fodak recruits, trains and supports .... based volunteers to work in the ....with disadvantaged groups and individuals.

9. Payne took very full advantage of the invitation .... by his cousin, who wanted somebody to cheer him up.

10. On really bad days Mae would come home absolutely ....

11. They were all very .... women, very well dressed with lots of jewelry.

12. You always hear aspiring authors .... about finding the time to write.

EXERCISE 45

SECTION A

Match these words with their synonyms and antonyms.

WORDS	SYNONYMS	ANTONYMS
1. REMAIN	----------------	----------------
2. TOGETHER	----------------	----------------
3. BEAUTY	----------------	----------------
4. IRRESISTIBLE	----------------	----------------
5. BROAD	----------------	----------------

SECTION B

These vocabularies in bold are wrongly used, correct them.

1. He's **agile** to serve in Margaret Thatcher's cabinet.

2. I need to **privilege** a new heavy coat.

3. Although he was very big he was incredibly **purchase** and elegant.

4. What are the basic entry **affirm** for the course?

5. We cannot **saddle** that this paint is genuine.

6. The company is **requirement** with an enormous amount of debt.

321. RECEPTIVE

Meaning and Examples:
Receptive means to be willing to listen to or accept ideas and suggestions.

a. I was happy to be speaking before such a *receptive* audience.
b. He was *receptive* to the idea of going back to school.

To understand more look it up in a dictionary. Then make your own sentences below.

1. _____.

2. _____.

3. _____.

322. BREAKTHROUGH

Meaning and Examples:
Breakthrough means a person's first important success after trying for a long period of time.

a. Researchers say they have achieved a major *breakthrough* in cancer treatment.
b. This job could be the *breakthrough* she's been waiting for.

To understand more look it up in a dictionary. Then make your own sentences below.

1. _____.

2. _____.

3. _____.

323. ADORE

Meanings and Examples:

1. To adore means to love or admire someone very much.
a. She *adores* her son.
b. He's a good doctor. All his patients *adore* him.

2. It also means to like or desire something very much or to take great pleasure in something.
He *adores* chocolate.

To understand more look it up in a dictionary. Then make your own sentences below.

1. _____.

2. _____.

3. _____.

324. PASSIONATE

Meaning and Examples:

To be passionate is, having, showing, or expressing strong emotions or beliefs for or toward something or someone.

a. She has a *passionate* interest in animal rights.
b. She is *passionate* about art/music/sports/healthy living.

To understand more look it up in a dictionary. Then make your own sentences below.

1. _____.

2. _____.

3. _____.

325. NOSTALGIA

Meaning:
Nostalgia is the pleasure and sadness that is caused by remembering something from the past and wishing that you could experience it again.

Example:
A wave of *nostalgia* swept over me when I saw my childhood home.

To understand more look it up in a dictionary. Then make your own sentences below.

1. _____.

2. _____.

3. _____.

326. QUITE

Meaning;
Quite means to a very noticeable extent or completely, entirely or exactly. It is used to express agreement.

Examples;
We go out to dinner quite frequently.
a. I haven't seen her for *quite* some time.
b. I am *quite* capable of doing it myself, thank you.
c. Winning this contest was *quite* an accomplishment.

To understand more look it up in a dictionary. Then make your own sentences below.

1. _____.

2. _____.

3. _____.

327. PRETTY

Meanings and Examples:
Pretty means to some degree or extent but not very or extremely.
a. The house was *pretty* big.
b. The movie was *pretty* good but not great.
c. She was driving *pretty* fast.

To understand more look it up in a dictionary. Then make your own sentences below.

1. _____.

2. _____.

3. _____.

328. RATHER

Meanings and Examples:
Rather is similar to quite and pretty. It is often used for negative ideas.
a. The weather isn't so good. It's *rather* cloudy.
b. Paul is *rather* shy, he doesn't talk very much.
c. He has been spending *rather* a lot of money lately.

Quite and pretty are also possible in these examples.
When rather is used for positive ideas, it means "unusually" or "surprisingly".
* These oranges are rather good. Where did you get them?

To understand more look it up in a dictionary. Then make your own sentences below.

1. _____.

2. _____.

3. _____.

329. FAIRLY

Meanings and Examples:

Fairly means to a reasonable or moderate extent.

Fairly is weaker than quite/rather/pretty.

If something is fairly good, it is not very good and it could be better.

a.   My room is *fairly* big, but I'd prefer a bigger one.

b.   We see each other *fairly* often, but not as often as we used to.

To understand more look it up in a dictionary. Then make your own sentences below.

1. _____.

2. _____.

3. _____.

330. HARDLY

Meanings:
1. It is used to say that something was almost not possible or almost did not happen.
2. It is also used to say that something happened for only a short time.

Examples:
a. She was *hardly* able to control her excitement.
b. *Hardly* a day goes by when I don't think about you.
c. The news is *hardly* a surprise.

Compare with "Not quite"
a. They haven't *quite* finished their meal yet.
b. I don't *quite/hardly* understand what you mean.
Look it up in a dictionary.

To understand more look it up in a dictionary. Then make your own sentences below.

1. _____.

2. _____.

3. _____.

TREASURE BOX 22: READ A LOT.

Read aloud in English for 15-20minutes every day. Research has shown it takes about three months of daily practice to develop strong mouth muscles for speaking a new language. Start with very simple books, even children books will help you.

331. RELATIVELY

Meaning:
Relatively means when compared to others that are similar.

Examples:
a.   The car's price is **relatively** high/low.
b.   There were **relatively** few people eat the meeting last night.
c.   This is a pretty good college, **relatively** speaking.
d.   We've had a **relatively** cold winter last year.

To understand more look it up in a dictionary. Then make your own sentences below.

1. _____ .

2. _____ .

3. _____ .

332. ABOUT

Meanings and Examples:
You use about when you mention what someone is saying, writing, or thinking.
a.   This book is **about** Japan.
b.   The movie was **about** a famous hero.

About can also mean **approximately** or **almost or nearly**.
a.   I am *about* 2 Kilometers from home.
b.   I ate *about* 3 cookies.

To understand more look it up in a dictionary. Then make your own sentences below.

1. _____ .

2. _____ .

3. _____ .

333. ABOVE

Meanings:
1. Above as a preposition means, in or to a higher place than something.
2. Also it means a greater in number, quantity, or size than something or more than something.
3. It may also means, having more importance or power than someone.

Examples:
a. He raised his arms *above* his head.
b. We rented an apartment *above* a restaurant.
c. Who is *above* him in that department?

To understand more look it up in a dictionary. Then make your own sentences below.

1. _____.
2. _____.
3. _____.

334. ACROSS

Meanings and Examples:
Across is a preposition and it means on the other side of something.
My friend's house is *across* the street from mine."
Another common meaning is from one side to the other.
They built a bridge *across* the river.
It may also means, throughout or in every part of a country, region etc.
The movie is now showing in theaters *across* America.

To understand more look it up in a dictionary. Then make your own sentences below.

1. _____.
2. _____.
3. _____.

335. ABILITY

Meanings:
Ability is a mental or physical power or skill or talent to do something.

Examples:
a.   His *ability* to dance was incredible."
b.   Some animals have the *ability* to run at speed of 96 kilometers per hour.
c.   Natural *ability* without education is like a tree without fruit.

To understand more look it up in a dictionary. Then make your own sentences below.

1.   _____.
2.   _____.
3.   _____.

336. CAPABLE

Meaning:
It means, able to do something, having the qualities or abilities that are needed to do something.

Examples:
a.   Many new cell phones are *capable* of connecting to the Internet.
b.   He is not *capable* of making those medical decisions himself.
c.   I don't believe that she's *capable* of murder.
d.   A storm is *capable* of causing widespread destruction.

To understand more look it up in a dictionary. Then make your own sentences below.

1.   _____.
2.   _____.
3.   _____.

337. BENEFIT

Meanings and Examples:

1. Benefit means a good point or to be useful or helpful to someone or something.

   A **benefit** of museum membership is that purchases are discounted.

2. It also means money that is paid by a company or by a government when someone dies, becomes sick, stops working etc.

   He began collecting his retirement **benefits** when he was 65.

3. Something extra such as vacation time that is given by an employer to workers in addition to their regular pay.

   The job doesn't pay much, but the **benefits** are good.

To understand more look it up in a dictionary. Then make your own sentences below.

1. _____.

2. _____.

3. _____.

338. BENEFICIARY

Meaning:

1. A person, organization, etc., that is helped by something or someone.
2. A person, organization, etc., that receives money or property when someone dies.

Examples:

a. She has made the school the sole *beneficiary* of her money and property in her will.
b. I am the *beneficiary* of your generosity."
c. Her father named her the *beneficiary* of his life insurance policy.

To understand more look it up in a dictionary. Then make your own sentences below.

1. _____.

2. _____.

3. _____.

339. OVER

Meaning:
Over is used where there is movement from one side to the other.
Also, over is used with a specified measurement or amount.

Examples:
a. I looked out of the window as we flew *over* Tokyo.
b. A notice *over* the door told us to remove our shoes.
c. Children *over* 12 have to pay the full price. at Tokyo Disney Resort
d. In the summer the temperature is often *over* 30 degrees.

To understand more look it up in a dictionary. Then make your own sentences below.

1. _____.

2. _____.

3. _____.

340. AFTER

Meanings and examples:
1. It means later in time.
    a. I'll finish my homework *after* dinner.
    b. *After* putting his book down, he switched off the light.
    c. She didn't get home till *after* midnight.

2. It also means "next to"
    a. Y comes *after* X.
    b. Turn right *after* the cinema.

3. It also means "as a result of"
    a. We won't be using the airline *after* all the trouble they caused us.

To understand more look it up in a dictionary. Then make your own sentences below.

1. _____.

2. _____.

3. _____.

EXERCISE 46

SECTION A

Write the synonyms and antonyms of the following words.

	SYNONYMS	**ANTONYMS**
1. COMPATIBLE	---------------	---------------
2. RECEPTIVE	---------------	---------------
3. BREAKTHOUGH	---------------	---------------
4. ADORE	---------------	---------------
5. PASSIONATE	---------------	---------------
6. NOSTALGIA	---------------	---------------

SECTION B

Complete the following sentences using
QUITE, PRETTY, RATHER, FAIRLY, RELATIVELY, HARDLY.

Combine with some of these words
(famous, good, hungry, late, noisy, often, old, surprise, a nice day, a lot of traffic, true, different, impossible, cloudy, boring) or your own idea.

1. I'm ....Is there anything to eat?

2. How are the photographs you took? ....better than usual.

3. I'm surprised you haven't heard of her. she's........................ famous.

250

4. I go to the cinema ....-may be once in a month.

5. I don't know when these houses were built, but they are ....

6. The weather isn't so good. it's.......................................

7. I didn't believe at first, but what he said was ....

8. I enjoyed the film, but it was ....

9. The journey took longer than I expected. There was ....

10. I'm afraid I can't do what you asked. It's ....

11. You can't compare the two things. They're...

12. The changes in service have .... been noticed.

341. GLOVE

Meaning:
This refers to something worn on a person's hand. It has a place for each finger. It is worn either for warmth or protection for the skin.

Examples:
a.   Every Christmas, she bought her mother a new pair of *gloves*.
b.   It is a good idea to wear rubber *gloves* when working with harsh cleaning products.

To understand more look it up in a dictionary. Then make your own sentences below.

1.   _____.

2.   _____.

3.   _____.

342. AGAINST

Meanings:
1. It means in opposition to someone.
2. It is also used to indicate the person or thing that is affected or harmed by something.
3. Also may mean," in competition with someone or something".

Examples:
a. Everyone was *against* them.
b. She voted *against* the proposal.
c. His parents were angry when they learned he had borrowed the car *against* their wishes.
d. He denies the charges that have been made *against* him.
e. It's the Yankees *against* the Red Sox tonight.

To understand more look it up in a dictionary. Then make your own sentences below.

1. _____.

2. _____.

3. _____.

343. ALONG

Meaning:
Along means, in the same direction as, or with the person or persons already mentioned.

Examples:
a. We walked *along* a narrow path in the forest.
b. He brought his son *along* with him.

To understand more look it up in a dictionary. Then make your own sentences below.

1. _____.
2. _____.
3. _____.

344. AMONG

Meaning:
This word may means, in or through a group of people or things.

Examples:
a. The disease spread quickly *among* the students forcing the school to close for two weeks.
b. She enjoys spending time at home *among* family and friends.
c. The property was divided equally *among* the four surviving children.

To understand more look it up in a dictionary. Then make your own sentences below.

1. _____.
2. _____.
3. _____.

345. BEYOND

Meanings and Examples:

1. Beyond means, on or to the far side of something or at a greater distance than something.
   The parking area is just *beyond* those trees.
2. Something that is beyond you is too difficult for you.
   The job is *beyond* his ability (the job is too difficult for him).
3. It may be used to say that something cannot be changed, understood, etc.
   The circumstances are *beyond* our control.
4. Something that continues after a period of time, a particular date, age, etc.
   The program is unlikely to continue *beyond* next year.

To understand more look it up in a dictionary. Then make your own sentences below.

1. _____.
2. _____.
3. _____.

TREASURE BOX 23: BE CURIOUS

Be **curious like children. Have interest** and **desire** to learn more. Use every opportunity to learn, such as when you are on the train, in the restaurant, change the signs from your language to English.

346. DUE TO

Meaning:
A situation is used to introduce the reason for a situation.

Examples:
a. Her health problem was **due to** overwork.
b. The train's delays are **due to** an electrical fault on the train line.
c. Classes were cancelled yesterday **due to** heavy snow.

To understand more look it up in a dictionary. Then make your own sentences below.

1. _____.

2. _____.

3. _____.

347. CARRY

Meaning:
This means to transport or to take something or someone from one place to another.

Examples:
a. He's over 80 years old and still *carries* himself erect/upright like a soldier.
b. "I will *carry* the groceries into the house for you."
c. "Could you please *carry* the baby for a while so I can rest my back?"

To understand more look it up in a dictionary. Then make your own sentences below.

1. _____.

2. _____.

3. _____.

348. CAUTION

Meaning:
Caution means carefulness or care taken to avoid danger or risk.

Examples:
a. "She used extreme *caution* when driving on the highway for the first time."
b. "Please use *caution* when you put the eggs in the fridge."
c. "You should use *caution* when operating the electric saw."

To understand more look it up in a dictionary. Then make your own sentences below.

1. _____.
2. _____.
3. _____.

349. CHARISMA

Meaning:
Charisma *is* personal characteristics which make a person able to attract, impress and inspire other people.

Examples:
a. "Because of his *charisma,* more than 200 people always showed up to his meetings."
b. "Her *charisma* was one of the things which caused them to offer her the position of manager."

To understand more look it up in a dictionary. Then make your own sentences below.

1. _____.
2. _____.
3. _____.

350. EXCLUDE

Meaning:
To prevent or leave out someone from doing something or being a part of a group.

Examples:
a. You can share files with some people on the network while *excluding* others.
b. The prices on the menu *exclude* tax.

To understand more look it up in a dictionary. Then make your own sentences below.

1. _____.
2. _____.
3. _____.

351. UNTIL

Meanings and Examples:
1. It is used to indicate the time when a particular situation, activity, or period ends.
   a. I stayed *until* morning.
   b. She will be out of the office *until* next week.
   c. The coupon is good *until* the end of March.

2. It is also used to indicate the time when something will happen, etc.
   a. We don't open *until* ten.
   b. The car won't be ready *until* tomorrow.

To understand more look it up in a dictionary. Then make your own sentences below.

1. _____.
2. _____.
3. _____.

352. DESSERT

Meaning:
Dessert is something sweet which is served at the end of a meal (Be careful not to confuse this with desert, such as the Sahara Desert.)

Examples:
a. "Fruit is a very healthy *dessert.*"
b. "Some of her favorite *desserts* are cake, cookies, ice cream, pie, and pudding."
c. "In the fall, some favorite *desserts* are pumpkin pie, apple crisp and caramel sundaes."

To understand more look it up in a dictionary. Then make your own sentences below.

1. _____.
2. _____.
3. _____.

353. FUTILE

Meaning:
This word means useless, having no result or effect.

Examples:
a. "Defying the law of gravity is *futile.*"
b. All our efforts to help him proved *futile.*
c. They made a *futile* [=vain] attempt to control the flooding.

To understand more look it up in a dictionary. Then make your own sentences below.

1. _____.
2. _____.
3. _____.

354. APPEAL

Meanings and Examples:
1. It may mean, to be liked by someone **or** to be pleasing or attractive to someone

*Pop music *appeals* to a wide variety of people.

2. It may also mean, to ask for something (such as help or support) in a serious way.

* The government *appealed* to the people to stay calm.

3. It may also mean, to make a formal request for a higher court to review and change decision.

*She lost the case, but she *appealed* the following month.

To understand more look it up in a dictionary. Then make your own sentences below.

1. _____.
2. _____.
3. _____.

355. UNDERESTIMATE

Meaning:
It means to think that something is less or lower than it really is, or that someone is less strong or less effective

Example:
Homeowners often *underestimate* the cost of repairing a roof.

To understand more look it up in a dictionary. Then make your own sentences below.

1. _____.
2. _____.
3. _____.

356. OUTRAGE

Meaning:
Outrage means, extreme anger or a strong feeling of unhappiness because of something bad, hurtful, or morally wrong.

Examples:
a. Many people expressed *outrage* at the court's decision.
b. Public *outrage* over the scandal was great.

To understand more look it up in a dictionary. Then make your own sentences below.

1. _____.

2. _____.

3. _____.

357. IMPULSE

Meanings and Examples:
1. To do something on (an) impulse or on a sudden impulse is to do it suddenly and without thinking about it first.
   a. He bought a new camera on *impulse*.
   b. She quit her job on a sudden *impulse*.

2. An impulse buy/purchase is something that is bought without thinking and that usually is not really needed
* Shopping with a credit card can lead to *impulse* buying.

To understand more look it up in a dictionary. Then make your own sentences below.

1. _____.

2. _____.

3. _____.

358. WITHOUT

Meanings:
Without means, not having or including (something).

Examples:
a. Do you take your coffee with or **without** sugar?
b. He went to the store **without** her.
c. They left **without** even saying goodbye.

To understand more look it up in a dictionary. Then make your own sentences below.

1. _____.

2. _____.

3. _____.

359. TOLERATE

Meanings:
To tolerate means to allow something that is bad or unpleasant to exist or be done.

Examples:
a. Our teacher will not **tolerate** bad grammar.
b. I can't **tolerate** that noise.
c. I don't like my boss, but I have to **tolerate** him.

To understand more look it up in a dictionary. Then make your own sentences below.

1. _____.

2. _____.

3. _____.

360. ACCURATE

Meaning:
Accurate means to be free from mistakes or errors.

Examples:
a. The model is *accurate* down to the tiniest details.
b. Her novel is historically *accurate*.
c. The machine is an *accurate* measuring device.

To understand more look it up in a dictionary. Then make your own sentences below.

1. _____.

2. _____.

3. _____.

TREASURE BOX 24: GOOD PRONUNCIATION IS IMPORTANT

Pronounce the ending of each word. Pay special attention to 'S' and 'ED' endings. This will help you strengthen the mouth muscles that you use when you speak English. You may not need the 'ED' when you become fluent, but you need them at the initial stage especially for spellings when you write.

EXERCISE 47

Choose the best prepositions from the brackets to fill in the gaps.

1. I enjoyed walking_____(round, in, over) the exhibition.

2. Look both ways before you walk_____(over, across, along) the road.

3. We sailed our boat_____(alongside, along, in)the river.

4. I studied the back of the man_____(behind, ahead of, beside) me in the queue.

5. Can you balance a book_____(on to, with, on top of) your head?

6. I couldn't find my name _____(in, on, throughout) the list.

7. Sally fell _____(off, over, down) the stairs and hurt her legs.

8. Do you prefer to sleep_____(on top of, on to, on) your back, your front or your side?

9. There was a CD enclosed _____(into, inside, in)the back cover of the book.

10. Dave climbed up_____(on to, on, above) the roof and rescued the kitten.

Exercise 48

Fill in the gaps with the appropriate words

of, for, on, in, at, with, to

1. We live in a little town which is not famous _____ anything.

2. Are you always fond _____American films?

3. He has been scared _____ heights since his accident

4. The streets will be crowded _____ tourists during the festival.

5. We didn't go on holiday. Jane wasn't very keen _____leaving her house.

6. Give me the name of the students who were responsible _____all that noise.

7. Why don't you trust me? Why are you suspicious _____ my intentions?

8. Ask my husband. I am not good _____repairing things.

9. My mother would hate being dependent _____ anybody.

10. Don't worry. We'll look after you. There's nothing to be scared _____.

11. I am sick of George ! He is always short _____money !

12. Look ! His handwriting is very similar _____mine.

13. He is a very honest man. We don't think he is capable _____ a theft.

14. We weren't interested at all _____ what he was telling about his journey.

15. The message he sent to me was full _____ mistakes.

361. BENEATH

Meaning:
In or to a lower position than something or someone or not worthy of or not good enough for someone.

Examples:
a.   The sky is above us and the earth is **beneath** us.
b.   Just **beneath** the surface of the water.
c.   He won't do any work that he considers **beneath** him.

To understand more look it up in a dictionary. Then make your own sentences below.

1.   _____.

2.   _____.

3.   _____.

362. DIVERSE

Meaning:
It means, made up of people or things that are different from each other.

Examples:
a.   His message appealed to a **diverse** audience.
b.   The group of students is very **diverse**.
c.   A **diverse** group of subjects.

To understand more look it up in a dictionary. Then make your own sentences below.

1.   _____.

2.   _____.

3.   _____.

363. SOURCE

Meaning:
A source is someone or something that provides something or its beginning.

Examples:
a. The college had its own power ***source.***
b. The team's bad play has been a ***source*** *of* disappointment.
c. The ***source*** of the Nile is very mall.

To understand more look it up in a dictionary. Then make your own sentences below.

1. _____.
2. _____.
3. _____.

364. FEATURE

Meaning:
It is an interesting or important part, quality, ability, etc. of something or somebody.

Examples:
a. This year's models include several new safety ***features.***
b. This camera has several ***features*** that make it easy to use.
c. Her eyes are her best ***feature.***

To understand more look it up in a dictionary. Then make your own sentences below.

1. _____.
2. _____.
3. _____.

365. CUSTOM

Meaning:
It means something made to fit the needs or requirements of a particular person.

Examples:
a. The new kitchen will have *custom* cabinets.
b. a *custom* furniture shop.

To understand more look it up in a dictionary. Then make your own sentences below.

1. _____.

2. _____.

3. _____.

TREASURE BOX 25: FILTER TO KEEP UP.

Try to understand the content of your conversation as a whole. Pick up the ones you understand especially the Subjects and the Verbs then try to speak while you mentally check your understanding.

EXERCISE 49

Write the synonyms and antonyms of the following words;

	SYNONYM	ANTONYM
1. RADIANT	....	....
2. CUSTOM	....	....
3. FEATURE	....	....
4. SOURCE	....	....
5. BENEATH	....	....
6. DIVERSE	....	....
7. ACCURATE	....	....
8. TOLERATE	....	....
9. WITHOUT	....	....
10. IMPULSE	....	....
11. OUTRAGE	....	....
12. UNDERESTIMATE	....	....
13. APPEAL	....	....
14. FUTILE	....	....
15. DESSERT	....	....

EXERCISE 50

Write the synonyms and antonyms of the following words;

	SYNONYM	**ANTONYM**
1. UNTIL	....	....
2. EXCLUDE	....	....
3. CHARISMA	....	....
4. CAUTION	....	....
5. CARRY	....	....
6. DUE TO	....	....
7. AGAINST	....	....
8. AMONG	....	....
9. ALONG	....	....
10. GLOVE	....	....
11. OVER	....	....
12. BENEFICIARY	....	....
13. BENEFIT	....	....
14. BEYOND	....	....
15. AFTER	....	....

Congratulations! You did it, you deserve a big treat!

Remember all the tips in the **treasure boxes** and this final one on **Speaking**:

How do you learn cycling? How do you learn swimming? You learn cycling by cycling and you learn swimming by swimming. **So, Speaking develops by speaking**. You may be making some grammar mistakes in English. You may not be confident. You may feel that your vocabulary is not good enough. But speaking develops your confidence in English. So, I would recommend that you find a native teacher or make friends with native English speakers, speak to as many people as possible in English every day speak or **cook** more and more sentences in English use your dictionary when you are not sure, learn **short useful phrases**, they will help develop your confidence and your speaking skills and then you will **connect**.

Happy learning!

Connect with the author at:
<u>englishconnect365seriesclub@yahoogroups.com</u>
or
<u>englishconnect365seriesclub@googlegroups.com</u>
or
<u>http://www.englishconnect365business.com/</u>

Check out other books in the series

ANSWERS TO THE EXERCISES

Exercises 1

1. Fever.
   b. A rise in the temperature of the body; frequently a symptom of infection.
2. Economy.
   b. The system of production and distribution and consumption
3. Smoke.
   c. A cloud of fine particles suspended in a gas.
4. To survive.
   a. Continue to live through hardship or adversity.
5. Ill
   c. Not healthy or sick.
6. To burn.
   a. To undergo rapid combustion or consume fuel in such a way as to give off heat.
7. Technique.
   c. A practical method or art applied to some particular task.
8. Bridge.
   b. A structure that allows people or vehicles to cross an obstacle such as a river or canal or railway etc.
9. To cross.
   b. To intersect or meet at a point.
10. Sudden.
    c. Happening without warning or in a short space of time.

Exercise 2

1. A movement from one place to another.
   c. Cross
2. A warning or intimation of something.
   c To notice

3. An expression of esteem, respect, affection, or admiration.
   a. Compliment
4. A person or thing that is unknown or with whom one is unacquainted.
   b. Stranger
5. To present as worthy of acceptance or trial.
   b. Recommend
6. To convey thoughts, opinions, or emotions orally.
   b. To speak up
7. To make known formally or officially.
   c. To declare
8. To put or set into, between, or among.
   c. To insert
9. Possessing great material wealth.
   c. Rich
10. Payment for labor or services to a worker, especially remuneration on an hourly daily, or weekly basis or by the piece.
    b. Wage

Exercise 3

1. Having a happy disposition; in good spirits.
   d. Cheerful
2. To seek advice or information.
   b. To consult
3. To manufacture or create economic goods and services.
   a. To produce
4. Not hypocritical or deceitful; open; genuine.
   c. Sincere
5. Free from showiness or ostentation; unpretentious
   c. Modest
6. Something useful that can be turned to commercial or other advantage
   a. Commodity.
7. To engage the services of (a person) for a fee.
   a. To hire
8. To give aid or support.
   b. To assist.

9. Degree or grade of excellence.
    b. Quality
10. To bring down amount, or degree; diminish.
    d. To reduce

Exercise 4

1. An angry dispute ; a disagreement marked by a temporary or permanent break in friendly relationship.
    c. Quarrel
2. To deduct a certain amount from a bill, charge, etc.
    c To discount
3. To breathe during sleep with hoarse or harsh sounds.
    b. To snore
4. To look with winking or half-shut eyes.
    b. Blink
5. To actively and attentively engaged in work or a pastime.
    a. Busy
6. Something offensive or annoying to individuals or to the community.
    c. Nuisance
7. Plain or undistinguished.
    c. Ordinary
8. A complete in natural growth or development, as plant and animal forms.
    b. Mature
9. An approximate judgment or calculation, as of the value, amount, time, size, or weight of something
    c. Estimate
10. 10. To give back or restore, especially money.
    a. Refund

Exercise 5

1. To observe carefully or critically.
    b. To Examine
2. To hold steadfastly to; cherish.
    c To Hug

3. Being in a state of putrefaction or decay; decomposed.
   a. Rotten
4. To plunge, especially headfirst, into water
   a. Dive
5. To use the nails or claws to dig or scrape at.
   c. To Scratch
6. Of a higher nature or kind.
   a. Quality
7. To expel air forcibly from the mouth and nose in an explosive action.
   a. To Sneeze
8. A space for storing goods.
   a. Storage
9. To emit or lose blood.
   b. To Bleed
10. A call to engage in a contest, fight, or competition.
    c. To Challenge.

Exercise 6 (Bonus exercise)

1. Go to the _____c_____ and try this dress on.
   [a] checkout
   [b] exchange
   [c] changing room

2. Look at the _____a_____ ! This shirt is too expensive. You can't afford it.
   [a] price tag
   [b] size
   [c] shopping list

3. I've lost my _____c_____ but I'd like to return this scarf. Is it possible?
   [a] afford
   [b] shopping list
   [c] receipt

4. I would like to return this electric kettle. Can I have a _____ b ____ ?
   [a] price tag
   [b] refund
   [c] checkout

5. May I try it on? - Yes, what _____ b _____ are you?
   [a] try on
   [b] size
   [c] shopper

6. I'd like to get a _____ a _____ for these shoes because they are too tight.
   [a] refund
   [b] size
   [c] try on

7. There was a big sale at that mall last week. Many _____ b _____ arrived at 4 a.m. to ensure a good place in line.
   [a] shopper
   [b] shoppers
   [c] fitting room

8. We go to the _____ b _____ because it sells products at lower prices.
   [a] changing room
   [b] discount store
   [c] afford

9. Henry lost his _____ c _____ and forgot to buy pork loin.
   [a] receipt
   [b] refund
   [c] shopping list

10. She worked on the _____a_____ at the supermarket last summer.
    [a] checkout
    [b] discount store
    [c] changing room

11. Have you got this dress in black? - Yes, we have. - Can I _____a____?
    [a] try it on
    [b] exchange
    [c] refund

12. I missed my train because I was queuing at the _____a_____ in a supermarket.
    [a] checkout
    [b] size
    [c] receipt

13. I bought this sweater yesterday but it's too small. Can I _____b_____ it please?
    [a] checkout
    [b] exchange
    [c] receipt

14. We don't have enough money. We aren't able to _____b_____ such expensive shoes.
    [a] exchange
    [b] afford
    [c] refund

15. Where can I try the jeans on? - The _____b___ is over there.
    [a] discount store
    [b] fitting room
    [c] price tag

16. This jacket _____b_____ you very well. I think you should buy it.
    [a] suit
    [b] suits
    [c] sizes

17. This tailcoat was very expensive but Ted could still _____c_____ it.
    [a] suit
    [b] refund
    [c] afford

18. You spend too much on clothes. Don't you look at the __b__ before buying something?
    [a] size
    [b] price tag
    [c] changing room

19. I'm going to buy her the blue dress. This color __a__ her best.
    [a] suits
    [b] tries on
    [c] refunds

20. If you don't like the color of the pullover, you can __c__ it. You'll get another one.
    [a] receipt
    [b] checkout
    [c] exchange

Exercise 7

1. Easy to approach, reach, enter, speak with, or use.
   a. Troublesome
   (b). Accessible
   c. Mature

2. To put into the mouth and draw upon
   a. To spot
   b. To stroll
   (c). To suck

3. Lacking definition; vague or indistinct.
   a. Ordinary
   b. Busy
   (c). Indecisive

4. To send from one person, thing, or place to another; convey.
   a. To sneeze
   (b). To transmit
   c. To compete

5. Full of distress or affliction.
   (a). Troublesome
   b. Challenge
   c. Accessible

6. Suited or favorable to one's comfort, purpose, or needs
   a. Collaborate
   b. Superior
   (c). Convenient

7. To work together, especially in a joint intellectual effort.
   a. To Spot
   (b). To collaborate
   c. To pronounce

8. 8. Lower someone's spirits; make downhearted
   a. To collaborate
   (b). To demoralize
   c. To transmit

9. To announce authoritatively or officially.
   (a). To pronounce
   b. To evaluate
   c. To deposit

10. To go for a leisurely walk
    (a). To Stroll
    b. To transmit
    c. To collaborate

Exercise 8

1. Different in nature or quality
   (a). Distinct
   b. Consult

2. An occupant or inhabitant of any place.
   a. Landlord
   (b). Tenant

3. To cause faster or greater activity
   (a). To accelerate
   b. To deposit

4. The opposite of landlady
   (a). Landlord
   b. Tenant

5. An itemized bill for goods sold or services provided
   a. Interest rate
   (b). Invoice

6. Subject to or under the authority of a superior
   (a). Subordinate
   b. Superior

7. The opposite of deposit.
    a.   To Evaluate
    (b). To withdraw

8. Uncertain, hazardous, or risky
    a.   Interest rate
    (b). Chancy

9. The items represented on a list, as a merchant's stock of goods.
    (a). Inventory
    b.   Evaluation

10. The act of pledging, or engaging oneself.
    a.   Distinct
    (b). Commitment

Exercise 9
Choose either (a) or (b) for the following definitions:

1. An increase, enlargement, or development, especially in the activities
    of a company.
    a.   Accelerate
    b.   Expansion

2. The specific percentage of total industry sales of a particular product
    achieved.
    a.   Market share
    b.   Interest rate

3. To arrange for or bring about by discussion and settlement of terms.
    a.   To evaluate
    b.   To negotiate

4. A verbal or written request, as for a job, etc
    a.   Application
    b.   Commitment

5. To keep in a specified, condition, state, position, etc.
   a. To transmit
   b. To maintain

6. The act of mentioning someone or something or a situation in speech or writing.
   a. reference
   b. maintain

7. when something is uncertain, hazardous, or risky.
   a. commitment
   b. chancy

8. A position of less power or authority than someone else.
   a. Subordinate
   b. reference

9. A detailed list of articles, giving the code number, quantity, and value of each.
   a. reference
   b. inventory

10. The state of being emotionally or intellectually devoted.
    a. commitment
    b. transmit

Exercise 10

1. A position, office, or place of accommodation that is unfilled or unoccupied
   (a). Vacancy
   b. Application

2. Something given or received in recompense for worthy behavior
   a. Expansion
   (b). Reward

3. Something added to complete a thing, make up for a deficiency
   a. Negotiate
   (b). Supplement

4. Unable to perform adequately; incompetent
   (a). Incapable
   b. Expansion

5. A statement about a person's qualifications, character, and dependability
   a. Application
   (b). References

6. To require or need as just, urgent, etc.
   (a). Demand
   b. Negotiate

7. The collective items or amounts of income of a person, a state, etc.
   a. Essential goods
   (b). Revenue

8. A person or organization designated by a company to solicit business on its behalf in a specified territory or foreign country.
   (a). Sales representative
   b. Essential goods

9. The execution or accomplishment of work, acts, feats, etc
   (a). Performance
   b. Demand

10. Basic goods or products necessary for everyday life.
    (a). Essential goods
    b. performance

Exercise 11

1. To require or need as just, urgent, etc.
   a. Demand
   b. Negotiate

2. The collective items or amounts of income of a person, a state, etc.
   a. a. Essential goods
   b. Revenue

3. A person or organization designated by a company to solicit business on its behalf in a specified territory or foreign country.
   a. Sales representative
   b. Essential goods

4. The execution or accomplishment of work, acts, feats, etc.
   a. Performance
   b. Demand

5. Basic goods or products necessary for everyday life.
   a. Essential goods
   b. performance

Exercise 12

A big ......**SUPPLIER**.......of essential goods have formed.....PARTNERSHIP.......
with some

smaller ones to ....**DONATE**........ goods and money to help the people affected in the recent earthquake and tsunami. They especially demanded a quicker step to make

sure that there is enough provision of ......**SAFETY**................. environment for all.

They also ....**HAMMERED**... on the quick control of the nuclear radiation and better alternative energy provision in the nearest future.

Exercise 13

1. **"What this generation must do is ....FACE.... its problems"**
   (John F. Kennedy).

2. **He is disliked by almost everyone because he is a ....LOAFER.....**

3. The government have decided to ....IMPLEMENT................ the new procedures.

4. She was very .....EAGER............ to go back to school.

5. Like all birds of prey, ...EAGLES...... have very large hooked beaks for tearing flesh from their preys strong muscular legs, and powerful talons.

6. Cities everywhere are banning plastic ......GROCERY...... bags, while one lonely California lawyer fights for their survival.

Exercise 14

1. The ability to move or be moved freely and easily.(**MOBILITY**)

2. In spite of the fact that or at the same time that something else is happening.(**WHILE**)

3. A number of vehicles so obstructed that they can scarcely move. (**TRAFFIC JAM**)

4. To contrive or plan beforehand or prearrange or predict.(**FERECAST**)

5. Throughout the course or duration of.(**DURING**)

6. To assist (somebody acting or reciting) by suggesting the next words or something forgotten or imperfectly learned.(**REMIND**)

Exercise 15

1. The situation .....**offered**.... us the opportunity to learn more.

2. The cabinet is ....**responsible**...... to the parliament.

3. There is a ......**lake**........ of spilled coffee on my desk

4. If anything ....**happens**.... to me it'll be your fault.

5. Degree centigrade is a **........unit....** of measurement for temperature.

6. A**.....library...........**is a place in which literary and artistic materials, such as books, periodicals, newspapers can be borrowed.

Exercise 16

1. The author **pushed her** latest book by making appearances in bookstores.

2. All citizens are equal before the **law**

3. The scandal **hurt** the candidate's chances for victory.

4. We shall never understand the natural **environment** until we see it as a living organism

5. Assembly line is a mechanical system in a **factory** whereby an article is conveyed through sites at which successive operations are performed on it.

6. We worked from **sunrise** to sunset.

Exercise 17

1. That doesn't sound related, it sounds**....foreign....**to the present discussion.

2. Many of the **..jobless....** moved to town is causing more competition.

3. She is **...currently...** working as a lab technician.

4. The union leaders are meeting to **...discuss...** about the fate of the factory.

5. They had decided to leave at **...dawn...** to be able to make their appointment.

6. The club's president **....recognized..** the new member.

Exercise 18

1. If a creditor has loaned money, performed services or provided a ..**debtor**.... with a product, that...**debtor**...has to pay the creditor.

2. You are asked to ...**refrain**... from smoking, drinking(alcohol) and eating in this hall.

3. The stereo and the refrigerator came with a three-year ...**warranty**.... but one year for the TV.

4. We bought .....**ticket**... for the opera I got one for over speeding on the way there.

5. She received some .....**polite**... applause despite the mistakes in her performance.

Exercise 19

1. We chose not to undertake the project because of the ....**enormous**..... costs involved.

2. I can't .....**smell**... anything because I'm so stuffed up.

3. After many years of war, people on both sides were longing for .... **peace**....

4. I offered the children a ......**bribe**.. for finishing their homework.

5. She has a new summer .....**wardrobe**........and she almost can't wait for summer to come.

6. The average American sees and hears thousands of ...**TV commercial**.. messages each day.

7. She treated her students with great ....**patience**..... and humor.

Exercise 20

1. They ....**pensioned him**....off when they found a younger man for the job.

2. There are fairy tales of searches for the pot of gold at the foot of the ....**rainbow**...

3. There's no greater ......**crime**..... than forgetting your anniversary.

4. The day's news coverage .....**focused**..... primarily/mainly *on* the scandal.

5. He was in ...**tears**......over the death of his dog.

6. The teacher ......**made**......her students memorize long lists of vocabularies.

7. A break in the cloud ......**let**...us see the top of the mountain.

8. The plate shattered when it ....**hit**........the floor.

Exercise 21

1. How can I ......**avoid**... paying too much tax?

2. His ideas are ....**attractive**...... *to* many people.

3. The project has ....**potential**... risks and advantages.

4. The trip turned out to be very ....**meaningful**... to both of them.

5. Aside from a few isolated ....**incident**..... the crowd was well-behaved.

6. The Chiba prefecture office distributed pamphlets ....**promoting**.. good dental hygiene.

Exercise 22

1. To go on board a vehicle for transportation. **EMBARK**

2. To complain quietly about something **or** to talk in an unhappy way. **GRUMBLE**

3. A place to which one is journeying or to which something is sent. **DESTINATION**

4. To start or engage, enlist, or invest in an enterprise. **EMBARK**

5. A group of people who support or believe in certain ideas. **CAMP**

6. To prevent or to forbid by authority from doing something. **PROHIBIT**

7. A place where athletes train before the beginning of a season. **CAMP**

8. To get out of a vehicle or craft. **DISEMBARK**

9. A place usually in the mountains or by a lake where young people can do different activities during the summer. **CAMP**

10. To go or to remove ashore out of a ship. **DISEMBARK**

Exercise 23

1. A year ago, both companies were in .....crisis....... but revived by government's aid.

2. "I'm so ...fatigued.... of your mother and her complaints about my food"

3. The company took ....aggressive........ steps to prevent illegal use of their equipment.

4. The program allows users to do ....global.......searches through all the available data.

5. They brought some bread to share as a ....demonstration.......... of goodwill.

6. Nancy wondered whether it was her ....destiny...... to live in England and marry Melvyn.

Exercise 24

1. lacking a normal or adequate supply of something specified. **POOR**

2. Easy to do or understand : not complicated: honest and open. **STRAIGHTFORWARD**

3. To end in a particular way or at a particular place. **TERMINATE**

4. To make (someone) more determined, hopeful, or confident. **ENCOURAGE**

5. Existing or functioning outside of the established society or offering or expressing a choice. **ALTERNATE**

6. Unusual or surprising : likely to be noticed. **REMARKABLE**

Exercise 25

1. A landlord may **.....retain...** part of your deposit if you break the lease.

2. She's not ashamed of her **......humble.....** beginnings.

3. The plans to rebuild Fukushima have been **...frustrated..** by bureaucratic delays.

4. The home team **....rallied.....** in the ninth inning to win the game.

5. The book puts these events in their proper historical and social **.... context.....**

6. He left his children a **..........legacy....** of love and respect.

Exercise 26

1. A specified way of thinking, feeling, acting or doing something. **MODE**

2. Very good or excellent : wonderful or very large or great. **TRMENDOUS**

3. To put (something) where people can see it or to show that you have (an emotion, quality, skill etc. **DISPLAY**

4. A spoken description of an event (such as a sports contest) as it is happening. **COMMENTARY**

5. pain and suffering or something that causes pain, suffering, or loss **HARDSHIP**

6. To catch up with; draw even or level with or to pass after catching up with. **OVERTAKE**

Exercise 27

1. He was too **astonished** to speak when he saw the present from his children.

2. The team's victory was **soured** by an injury to one of their best players.

3. Generous people regularly give money and donate clothes to help the **needy**.

4. High interest rates are **prolonging** the economy recession.

5. Everyone screamed as the plane suddenly went into a **nosedived**.

6. They've reduced the number of **personnel** working on the project.

Exercise 28
Choose the best word for the following definitions:

1. Possible to be easily broken or damaged.
   a. Fever
   b. To notice
   (c). Fragile

2. To seize temporarily or permanently as way of penalty for use.
   a. Technique
   (b). Confiscate
   c. To notice

3. To ignore (something) or treat (something) as unimportant.
   a. Compliment
   (b). Disregard
   c. To recommend

4. A situation in which many people do not have enough food to eat.
   (a). Famine
   b. Stranger
   c. Economy

5. To think about something unceasingly or persistently.
   a. Rich
   b. Recommend
   (c). Obsess

Exercise 29

1. He told us a story __**involving**__ life on a farm.

2. A piece of food __**obstructed**_____ his airway and caused him to stop breathing.

3. She became very __**remote**_____ in her old age.

4. The moderator's role is to _**facilitate**_ the discussion by asking appropriate questions.

5. He is an ___**obstinate**___ child with a violent temper.

6. He shows a high level of ___**proficient**___ in Spanish.

Exercise 30

1. There was an immediate ---**outbreak**--- of paper shuffling and a pretense of work when the supervisor passed through the room.

2. Honesty, truth and justice are --**abstract**---- words.

3. They are working hard to ---**impress**--- the value of money on their children.

4. It has been more than six years since the fall of the Taliban, fewer than 30% girls are --**eligible**---to enroll in schools.

5. Lack of experience is a major -----**obstacle**-- for her opponent.

6. The article discusses a number of ways people can----**boost**--- their immune systems.

Exercise 31

Beggar Replacement
The doorbell rang, and the housewife answered it. She found two beggars outside. "So, you're begging in twos now?!" she exclaimed." No, only for today," one of them replied. "I'm showing my replacement the ropes before going on holiday."
Make the best choice.

1. A 'beggar' is a person who.......
    a. sells food and clothes
    b. has no money
    c. **asks for money**
    d. does the housework

2. To 'exclaim' means to..........
   a. say something kindly
   b. say suddenly and loudly
   c. walk quickly
   d. look angrily

3. A .... is a person that you put in place of yourself or another.
   a. beggar
   b. rope
   c. housewife
   d. replacement

4. 'Ropes' here means ....
   a. the rules and customs in a place or activity
   b. pieces of strong thick cord
   c. people you probably meet in a special place
   d. houses which are expensive

5. 'Reply' means...................
   a. to take someone for a ride
   b. to ignore someone
   c. to respond in words or writing
   d. to make a loud noise

6. 'found' here means
   a. to invent something
   b. to gain or regain the use or power of something
   c. to be determined
   d. to come upon or see often accidentally

Exercise 32

1. The ___suspect___vehicle was reported to the police.

2. They were unable to prevent bacteria from __infecting_ the wound.

3. His essay ___contrasts__ his life in America with/to life in India.

4. She never fully recovered from the ___trauma_ she suffered during her childhood.

5. He doesn't write _legibly_ at all and it is very difficult to read his writings.

6. The social/political/religious __dimensions__ of the problem must also be taken into account.

Exercise 33

A Hotel Experience

I was Staying at a hotel in Kawaguchi, Japan. I couldn't sleep because the television in the residents' lounge was so loud. As I could see from the top of the stairs, the lounge was in total darkness, so I crept downstairs in my pajamas. I went to the TV and after some fumbling with the knobs I managed to switch it off.

As I turned to leave, I suddenly became aware of a semi-circle of people sitting in the dark who, up until that moment, had been enjoying a television program.

1. 'Lounge' is..........
   (c) Public sitting room in a hotel.

2. To 'creep' means to ....
   (d). move quietly

3. To '.......' means to move the hands awkwardly to do something or to find something.
   (a). fumble

4. A 'knob' is a .....
   (c).round handle

5. Aware here means ....
   (b). having knowledge or conscious of something.

6. Resident means.............

   (a). One who lives or resides in a particular place permanently or for an extended period.

7. Semi circle means..........................

   (c). a half of a circle

Exercise 34

1. A very short period of time.....**Instant.**

2. To forbid someone from doing or being part of something...**Ban.**

3. Extreme mental or physical pain.....**Agony.**

4. Responsible for committing a crime or doing something bad or wrong...**Guilty.**

5. To stop someone or something from doing something...**Prevent.**

6. To make something sure, certain, or safe...**Ensure.**

Exercise 35

1. To impose (a course of action) upon a person or a group of people is ....to....**enforce**................

2. To make suitable to requirements or conditions; adjust or modify fittingly is ....to...**adapt.**......

3. To express or feel disapproval, dislike, or distaste is ..to...**object**........

4. Large in scale, amount, or degree is ....to be **massive**........

5. Important or having or likely to have influence or effect is ....to be **significant**.........

6. of strange, odd or extraordinary character is ....to be **weird**..............

Exercise 36

1. Required or commanded by authority; obligatory ---**mandatory**-------

2. To assign or entrust responsibility or authority to another ----**to delegate**----

3. The collecting of information about a particular subject ----**to research**----

4. Someone or something that people talk or write about ----**a topic**-----

5. To provide what is useful or necessary -----**to aid**-----------

6. A strong and harmful need to regularly have something or do something -**addiction**---

Exercise 37

Match the following words with the appropriate definitions.
TREATMENT, UNDERGROUND, VANISH, NOMINEE, REVIVE, PROPOSAL

1. To disappear, especially suddenly or mysteriously. **VANISH**
2. To bring back or to return to life or consciousness. **REVIVE**
3. The act, manner, or method of handling or dealing with someone or something. **TREATMENT**
4. A person or organization named to act on behalf of someone else. **NOMINEE**
5. something offered as new offerings for investors included several index funds. **PROPOSAL**
6. Hidden or concealed or relating to an organization involved in secret or illegal activity. **UNDERGROUND**
   How did you do?

Exercise 38

1. The action for which a person or thing is particularly fitted or employed. **FUNCTION**

2. Following in time or order; succeeding. **SUBSEQUENT**

3. Capable of being bent repeatedly without injury or damage. **FLEXIBLE**

4. To cause to diminish, as in strength, value, or quality. **IMPAIR**

5. The quality of being widely honored and acclaimed; fame. **RENOWN**

6. A condition or place of great disorder or confusion. **CHAOS**

Exercise 39

1. Higher education always seems to ....**generate**........... controversy.

2. The horse ....**stumbled**...... and almost fell.

3. These ideas are no longer ....**obtainable**..... for our generation.

4. The downfall of the company was brought about by many .... **negligence**......of the staff.

5. He decided to...........**abstain**........ from taking part in the discussion.

6. I was impressed by the calm and ....**professional**..... way she handled the crisis.

Exercise 40
Possible same options

1. UNLIKELY ------- **Not likely, improbable, Not promising, likely to fail.**

2. TO DILUTE -------- **weaken, adulterate, decrease, lessen**

3. TO BOND -------**fix, hold, bind, connect, glue, stick, paste, fasten**

4. TO GAMBLE ------**take a chance, back, speculate, bet.**

5. ASSET ----------benefit, help, service, aid, advantage, strength

6. RADIANT ------------glow, happy, joyful

Exercise 41

WORDS	SYNONYMS	ANTONYMS
1. MANIPULATE	use	Leave alone
2. INTIMIDATE	bully	encourage
3. SYNONYM	equivalent	antonym
4. ANTONYM	opposite	synonym
5. COMPENSATE	refund	deprive
6. SPECIFIC	definite	uncertain

Exercise 42

1. To notice, think or become aware of something or someone is to **perceive**

2. The way something happens or the specific details of an event is the **circumstance**

3. To see, find, or become aware of something for the first time is to **discover**

4. To continue to be or to live or to be real is to **exist**

5. Easy to understand or recognize or visible is to **manifest**

6. Producing a result that is wanted or having an intended effect is to be **effective**

7. A particular way of explaining or understanding events is.**narrative.**

Exercise 43

	SYNONYM	**ANTONYM**
1. RESOLUTION	..STRONG DECISION....	..FRUSTRATION..
2. BEGINNING	....COMMENCEMENT	...TERMINAL.....
3. INFLUENCE	.....AUTHORITY......	..INSIGNIFICANT.
4. HAMMER	......REPEAT.	...WITHDRAW
5. ATTITUDE	........PERSPECTIVE.......	....
6. MOMENTUM	.....IMPULSE	...SLOW....
7. TMID	...FEARFUL..	...BRAVE...
8. IGNITE	...START UP.....	...QUENCH...
9. ENCOUNTER	...CONFRONTAION....	...RETREAT...
10. HENCEFORTH	...FROM NOW.....	..PRECEDE..
11. PARTICIPATE	...JOIN IN..........	......OBSERVE......
12. TRADITIONAL	...COMMON.....	......NEW.......

Exercise 44

1. She ....**occupies**.... herself with her butterfly collection.

2. Dr. Jones ......**emphasizes**....... exercise in addition to a change in diet.

3. Paul was a shy, pleasant ...**solitary**.... man, his evenings were spent in ..solitary... drinking.

4. Relief agencies say the .....**immediate**.. problem is not a lack of food, but transportation.

5. The trip has been ....**Postponed**......... twice.

6. The governor found it .....**presumptuous**.. that the mayor called him by his first name.

7. Live animal research is more tightly ..**regulated**... in Britain than anywhere else in the world.

8. Fodak recruits, trains and supports ..**community**.. based volunteers to work in the ..**community**.. with disadvantaged groups and individuals.

9. Payne took very full advantage of the invitation ..**extended**... by his cousin, who wanted somebody to cheer him up.

10. On really bad days Mae would come home absolutely ....**shattered**..

11. They were all very ....**flamboyant**.. women, very well dressed with lots of jewelry.

12. You always hear aspiring authors .....**lament**... about finding the time to write.

Exercise 45

<u>SECTION A</u>

<u>WORDS</u>	<u>SYNONYMS</u>	<u>ANTONYMS</u>
1. REMAIN	Stay, Rest, continue	Leave, Depart
2. TOGETHER	With, Join	Solely, Independent

3. BEAUTY	Loveliness, Merit	Merit, Ugliness
4. IRRESISTIBLE	Seductive, tempting	repulsive, unappealing
5. BROAD	Expansive, Wide	Narrow

SECTION B

1. He's *privilege* to serve in Ronald Regan's cabinet.

2. I need to *purchase* a new heavy coat.

3. Although he was very big he was incredibly *agile* and elegant.

4. What are the basic entry *requirements* for the course?

5. We cannot *affirm* that this paint is genuine.

6. The company is *saddled* with an enormous amount of debt.

Exercise 46

SECTION A
Write the synonyms and antonyms of the following words.

	SYNONYMS	ANTONYMS
1. COMPATIBLE	adaptable/suitabbe	incompatible/ antagonistic
2. RECEPTIVE	accessible/friendly	insensitive/unfriendly
3. BREAKTHOUGH	discovery/sudden success	setback/set backward
4. ADORE	worship/cherish	Hate/abhor/condemn

5. PASSIONATE	desireous/loving	indifferent/impassionate
6. NOSTALGIA	fond memories/reminiscence	apathetic/regret/anticipation

SECTION B

1. I'm ...**quite /..pretty** hungry.... Is there anything to eat?

2. How are the photographs you took? ...**Relatively**.....better than usual.

3. I'm surprised you haven't heard of her...she's........quite/pretty...... famous.

4. I go to the cinema .....**quite often/ a lot**..........-may be once in a month.

5. I don't know when these houses were built, but they are ......**relatively/ fairly** old.......

6. The weather isn't so good. it's ....**rather** cloudy.

7. I didn't believe at first, but what he said was ....**quite** true....

8. I enjoyed the film, but it was ....**quite/ relatively** boring..

9. The journey took longer than I expected. There was ....**quite** a lot of traffic........

10. I'm afraid I can't do what you asked. It's ....**rather** impossible..........

11. You can't compare the two things. They're ......**quite** different...............

12. The changes in service have ....**hardly**........ been noticed.

Exercise 47

1. I enjoyed walking____**round**_____the exhibition.

2. Look both ways before you walk_**across**____the road.

3. We sailed our boat_____**along**___the river.

4. I studied the back of the man__**ahead of**_____me in the queue.

5. Can you balance a book_____**on top of**__ your head?

6. I couldn't find my name _**on**__the list.

7. Sally fell ____**down**__ the stairs and hurt her legs.

8. Do you prefer to sleep _____**on**_ your back, your front or your side?

9. There was a CD enclosed __**inside**_____ the back cover of the book.

10. Dave climbed up__**on to**_____ the roof and rescued the kitten.

Exercise 48

1. We live in a little town which is not famous __**for**____ anything.

2. Are you always fond __**of**_____ American films?

3. He has been scared ____**of**__ heights since his accident

4. The streets will be crowded ___**with**____ tourists during the festival.

5. We didn't go on holiday. Jane wasn't very keen __**in/at**_____ leaving her house.

6. Give me the name of the students who were responsible ____**for**__ all that noise.

7. Why don't you trust me? Why are you suspicious __**of**_ my intentions?

8. Ask my husband. I am not good __at__ repairing things.

9. My mother would hate being dependent _____on__ anybody.

10. Don't worry. We'll look after you. There's nothing to be scared __of_.

11. I am sick of George ! He is always short __of_ money !

12. Look! His handwriting is very similar __to__ mine.

13. He is a very honest man. We don't think he is capable __of_ a theft.

14. We weren't interested at all _in__ what he was telling us about his journey.

15. The message he sent to me was full __of__ mistakes.

Exercise 49

	SYNONYM	**ANTONYM**
1. RADIANT	...glowing...	...gloomy...
2. CUSTOM	..tradition......	.....untraditional..
3. FEATURE	...characteristics....	...unrelated.....
4. SOURCE	...origin......	......terminal...
5. BENEATH	..below........	...above......
6. DIVERSE	.......various....	......similar......
7. ACCURATE	...correct........	......wrong.....
8. TOLERATE	...endure......	......prohibit........

9. WITHOUT	...lacking......	......satisfy...
10. IMPULSE	......momentum.....	...indifferent......
11. OUTRAGE	...anger.........	......calm.........
12. UNDERESTIMATE	.....undervalue.....	......overstate.....
13. APPEAL	......plead....	.........reject......
14. FUTILE	......useless......	......effective......
15. DESSERT	...sweet course....	......non sweet......

Exercise 50

	SYNONYM	**ANTONYM**
1. UNTIL	...before.....	......after.........
2. EXCLUDE	...forbid.........	.........allow......
3. CHARISMA	...attraction.........	......disgust......
4. CAUTION	......alertness.....	......recklessness...
5. CARRY	...lift........	......drop......
6. DUE TO	...because of......	.........no reason......
7. AGAINST	......hostile........	.........favorable......

8. AMONG	......with........	........separate........
9. ALONG	......next to......	......against........
10. GLOVE	......mitt......	......sock........
11. OVER	......above..........	......below.....
12. BENEFICIARY	...recipient.....	...payee.........
13. BENEFIT	......gain...	......loss......
14. BEYOND	...past......	...same level......
15. AFTER	......following........	......before.........

INDEX

A

B

C

31. COMMERCIAL
84. COMMITMENT
34. COMMODITY
307. COMMUNITY
320. COMPATIBLE
276. TO COMPENSATE
26. COMPETITIVE
9. COMPLIMENT
197. CONFISCATE
32. CONSULT
181. CONTEXT
220. CONTRAST
65. CONVENIENT
152. CRIME
166. CRISIS
4. CROSS
37. CRUEL
134. CURRENTLY
365. CUSTOM

D

130. DAWN
18. DECLARE
246. DELEGATE
96. DEMAND
170. DEMONSTRATE
71. TO DEMORALIZE
74. DEPOSIT MONEY
352. DESSERT
163. DESTINATION
167. DESTINY
346. DUE TO
268. DILUTE
219. DIMENSION
56. DISCOUNT
278. TO DISCOVER
131. TO DISCUSS
164. DISEMBARK
187. DISPLAY

M

247. MANDATORY
86. TO MAINTAIN
280. TO MANIFEST
272. TO MANIPULATE
87. MARKET SHARE
240. MASSIVE
44. MATURE
157. MEANINGFUL
112. MOBILITY
188. MODE
36. MODEST
290. MOMENTUM
25. MULTINATIONAL COMPANY

N

291. NARRATIVE
190. NEEDY
266. NEGLIGENCE
89. TO NEGOTIATE
252. NOMINEE
195. NOSEDIVE
325. NOSTALGIA
11. NOTICE
42. NUISANCE

O

237. TO OBJECT
200. OBSESS
207. OBSTACLE
206. OBSTINATE
204. TO OBSTRUCT
261. TO OBTAIN
297. OCCUPY.
120. TO OFFER
40. ORDINARY
209. OUTBREAK
356. OUTRAGE

R

271. RADIANT
149. RAINBOW
182. RALLY
328. RATHER
321. RECEPTIVE
132. RECOGNIZE / RECOGNISE
16. RECOMMEND
30. REDUCE
90. REFERENCES
137. REFRAIN
54. REFUND
303. REGULATE
331. RELATIVELY
308. REMAIN
176. REMARKABLE
201. REMOTE
259. RENOWN
218. REPLACE
213. REPLY
316. REQUIREMENT
243. RESEARCH
230. RESIDENT
293. RESOLUTION
121. RESPONSIBLE
180. RETAIN
98. REVENUE
253. TO REVIVE
91. REWARD
19. RICH
61. ROTTEN

S

317. SADDLE
104. SAFETY
97. SALES REPRESENTATIVE
60. TO SCRATCH
227. SEMICIRCLE

T

Did you enjoy the book?
Check out other books here: http://www.englishconnect365business.com/
Or Kindle/PDF versions on amazon etc. and remember to leave a review.

Join the club: englishconnect365seriesclub@yahoogroups.com
and connect with the author for regular information and feedback
You can also email the author at : englishconnect365seriesclub@gmail.com

Printed in the United States
By Bookmasters